Abled Tales

Kashmira Adil Kakalia

notionpress.com

INDIA · SINGAPORE · MALAYSIA

ISBN
Hardcase 979-8-89929-877-6
Paperback 979-8-89777-689-4

Dedication

To my ever-loving family

To my students and my clients

To Ahura Mazda, who makes it all possible.

Contents

Acknowledgements

This book is a product of passion. Products of love always come into being with the support of several individuals. My ever-supportive husband, Adil, guides me in evaluating critical decisions, encourages me to improve, and always stands by my side.

My daughter, Urveez, has been my hero and is an inspiration to me. This book jumpstarted once she encouraged me to write blogs for our website, www.ImPerfect.co.in.

Special thanks to Urveez, my great proofreader. With her super skills and talent, she has edited this book. She has an eye for detail and has guided me towards making my content comprehensible to all my dear readers. Thank you, my dear editor.

A big thank you to Mithra; she has made this book more attractive with all the illustrations you will encounter. When I approached Mithra to be the illustrator for my book, she readily agreed even before knowing what this book was all about. I truly appreciate the artwork and her promptness.

Her interpretations and depictions of concepts truly enhance the stories you will experience.

A big thank you to Sooni Taraporevala for writing a foreword for my first book, 'Abled Tales'. Sooni has been an inspiration to me. She has many awards to her credit, including a Padma Shri. She has authored many books. She is a screenwriter, a photographer, a publisher, and a filmmaker. She is a loving daughter, a wonderful wife, and a doting mother. Most of all, she is a humble person. I truly appreciate your efforts. I am truly honoured and ever so grateful.

My ever-supportive family, my parents, my parents-in-law—the list is endless. My mornings are frequently off to a pleasant start when I receive photographs or clippings of my writings in the newspaper over our family groups.

The gift of great mentors is a true blessing. I see it as an endowment of luck. It is the reason why my learning was elevated, my career was lengthened, and my life was meaningful. The institutions where I studied, educated, volunteered, and trained housed my encouraging and nurturing teachers and mentors.

My friends and colleagues with whom I worked for about three decades formed my family, a place I called my second home. They taught me the meaning of joy at work.

My friends and colleagues with whom I trained in narrative therapy helped me recapture the magic of stories.

To all my students, the youngest ones, young adults, adults, and seniors, with whom I associate as a teacher, a counsellor, a friend, or a guide, this book would not be possible without them.

To my students and parents, young and old, who have shared their stories of determination and resilience in this book.

To every one of you, my dear readers who have read this book.

With encouragement and support from my better half, I began my private practice confidently. I was able to serve and guide many more individuals. I teamed up with my daughter, who is the founder of ImPerfect. ImPerfect is dedicated to providing ethical, relevant, theoretically guided, and empirically driven Mental Health Services.

Foreword

Kashmira Kakalia's book is a much-needed insight into the invisible world of mental health in India. There is so much stigma associated with this topic that Kashmira's first chapter is "Dealing with Stigma". In a country so obsessed with "log kya kahenge" or "what will people say", this book is a must-read to break that mindset that cripples us and our children.

Written simply, without any jargon, Kashmira has distilled her 30 years of experience into a book that is easy to read and follow by the layperson who is not in the mental health field. It deals with issues faced by a range of people, from young kids to seniors, and shows us how to understand them and deal with them correctly and thoughtfully. It also shows parents and teachers how to identify strengths, improve self-confidence, reduce social anxiety, and improve academic performance.

Filled with case studies of children from all economic backgrounds and their parents, this book has something for everyone. From how words matter to dealing with trauma, learning disabilities, language barriers, narrative therapy, and strategies to overcome self-doubt, this book teaches us how to be humane, whether or not we have differently abled people in our immediate circles.

The testimonials at the end of the book are heartwarming. Kashmira has helped countless children and parents, and this book will hopefully reach and help many more.

– **Sooni Taraporevala**

Introduction

30years! It does seem like aeons ago. My journey as a special needs teacher and a mental health professional began interestingly. It so happened that as college students, we at home were encouraged to use our long holiday breaks fruitfully. So, my sister and I would take up simple jobs to earn pocket money. I graduated and came in touch with an organisation that was raising funds, and they offered 25 per cent of the amount collected to us. Wow! That seemed like a lot of money. It was not an easy task, but I did earn good money. But more than money, I bonded with the institute and the kids there. I realised what I meaningfully wanted to do with my life and how passionate I was. I studied for my Bachelor's in Special Education, and the journey continues.

Kids are the most lovable, gullible, and mouldable. You know the feeling when you are young, new to the field, and excited as a fresh graduate with a new job—new ideas, new thoughts. I was lucky I was trusted with the freedom to experiment.

30 years ago, the awareness of specific learning disabilities was negligible. It was a challenge blended with spades of learning. There was a heap of stigma, a lack of awareness, and a denial of the difficulties, more so as the "disability" was invisible.

Sadly, even three decades on, we as therapists are still striving to eliminate the stigma attached and raise awareness to create an accepting and inclusive society.

We may have heard of a lot of famous personalities worldwide who have struggled with dyslexia and contributed to raising awareness in society.

Working as a special educator, I was not just dealing with kids and their struggles with academics. Teachers associated with the kids had to be trained to be empathetic to different ways of learning. Parents needed to be involved, counselled, and encouraged to accept, understand, and motivate their kids by setting realistic goals.

I realised the need for a professional approach to counselling, so I completed my diploma in Narrative Practices.

Over the years, I have grown with enriching experiences and satisfactory results. Every student I have taught has made me humble and taught me so much. Most of them are settled in life and doing very well for themselves. I will not be honest here if I do not mention that there were circumstances when a few students had to be assigned to different boards of study depending on individual capacities and levels of functioning.

Many times, the school authorities make decisions based on school policies.

I toyed with the idea of penning down my experiences through the years. Finally (after much persuasion), I got to it.

This book is for everyone. I have worked with all age groups and have shared three decades of my experiences here. It would be a good read for educators, parents, grandparents, and therapists.

I mentioned famous personalities earlier; well, some of my kids are famous too. As I share my experiences and knowledge, I will not mention the names of my students. All the names used in this book are fictitious, and they only partially resemble an individual to maintain their privacy as I continue sharing our journey. Over the decades, I may have encountered many students and clients with similar concerns. Some stories may have a blend of a few different individuals' concerns to share my learnings concisely and to prevent repetition. While you go through the book, if you feel like you identify with a person in a story, it may be so by happenstance. Not a single story reflects any individual in an identifiable way.

This book intends to share what I have learned from my practices, share the power of resilience, and, most importantly, spread awareness and create an inclusive environment in society. The chapters in this book reflect the challenges and guidance towards therapy to extend support to fellow beings. I frequently invite the reader to join me in reflecting on what they are reading. Self-awareness, through reflection and insight, is imperative to change. If you find yourself feeling uncomfortable while you engage with the stories you encounter here or during the reflective prompts, sit with it and feel it transform you, rather than running away.

The 'abled' in this book may not have changed the world! But each of them has certainly changed me, and for that, I am grateful.

A Note on Terminology

In our chapter, 'Our Words Matter', we will discuss in detail how important our words are when spoken to address someone. The words we use have a significant effect on others around us.

Throughout this book, you will come across certain words frequently. You may notice that they are mentioned differently in different places, even in the same story. You may come across terms like "dyslexic" as a part of a story. It may be mentioned like this to reflect the treatment one receives in society. However, this is highly stigmatising language and must be steered clear of. One should avoid labelling persons with disabilities with their diagnoses and instead address them as 'person with dyslexia' or 'has dyslexia'.

This is what is referred to as 'People-First Language' (PFL). It places the person before the disability to describe what a person has and not who a person is. This is to emphasise that the person is not defined by the condition and should be treated with respect and dignity (Wooldridge, 2023).

Try to use PFL in daily life, no matter what concern you are referring to, whether you are referring to someone with invisible disabilities like a learning difficulty, mental health distress, or neurodivergent concerns, or someone with visible physical disabilities or sensory-motor difficulties.

This is also especially important because a greater degree of 'disability' comes from the way our physical world is designed to serve only the normative, neurotypical, and physically typical individuals who make up the 'majority'. The use of appropriate terminology is important to avoid exclusion and discrimination. It is essential that people are treated with respect. It shows that you value them.

Warning! Terms like handicapped, crippled, mentally retarded, deaf, can't see, are outdated. They are considered disrespectful. An expression like 'differently abled' also causes concern; instead, using the term 'persons with disabilities' is encouraged.

Before we begin, we want to share that we (the author and editor) are always learning, too. We may humanly falter despite our best efforts, and we acknowledge and learn from that.

Reflections for the reader:

Dear readers, take a break and put this book aside. Take a deep breath in and slowly let your breath out. Take one more breath in, and slowly exhale. Gently close your eyes. Imagine you are in a vehicle sitting beside the driver, and you see a person who cannot see is about to cross the road. What would you tell the driver? Please drive slowly, someone ___________________________ is crossing the road.

You move ahead and you see a person using a wheelchair seeking help. You say, "Stop the vehicle, someone ___________________________ needs help."

You reached your destination. You are content. You used the correct terminology. You may open your eyes. :)

Imagine if:

You are at a coffee shop, waiting in line to place your order at the counter. The person in front of you seems to be taking an impossibly long time to place their order. The barista is getting impatient with the customer because he doesn't understand what the customer seems to be communicating. The barista glances at you for assistance. You shrug helplessly, as clueless as the barista himself.

The barista from the next counter notices. She steps up after finishing with the customer she was serving. She swiftly moves her arms and hands in the air, but purposefully. You don't understand, nor does the barista before her. The customer's face brightens up! His shoulders relax, and his body gets comfortable. He responds to the barista by moving his arms and hands, too! They communicate using the same language: sign language! He receives his order, seems to engage in a 'quiet' small talk with the barista, and enjoys his meal. The little child in the line behind you tells his mum, "Why don't they teach us their language in school, too? We are already learning English, Hindi, Marathi, and French anyway," quickly types on his phone and continues speaking, "Wow, mum… more than 70 million people use sign language around the world."

Would you call the previous interaction a language barrier or ignorance?

How come it is always easier for kids to question the premise: 'Just because it works for the majority, it doesn't make it right?'

Chapter One

Dealing with Stigma

Sam lived with his parents in a cottage. This family of three had few friends. They rarely met other family members. Sam had started attending his school. His peers did not like to sit beside him. They said he was awkward. His parents feared being humiliated and took him out of school. They interacted with a few people, and their outings were limited to the market and work. Even at work, one would not hear them speak about their son. Sam was not the only boy who faced such humiliation or was labelled awkward. His parents wanted the best for him. But shame took over, and they preferred to seclude themselves from society.

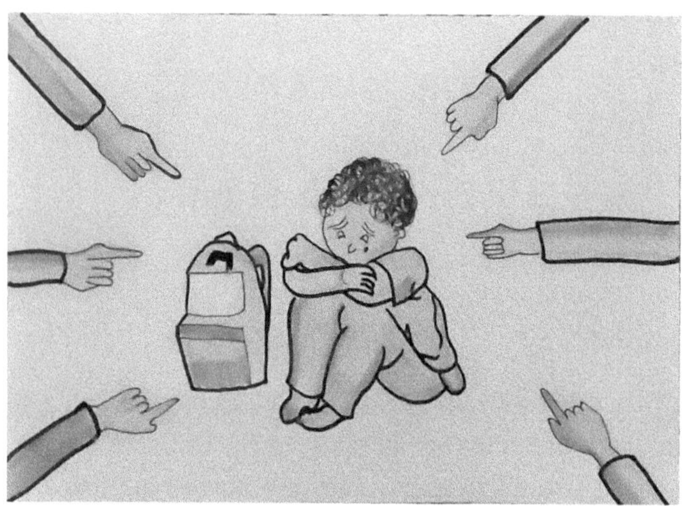

Dear readers, does this story sound familiar, or do you think they overreacted? Have you ever knowingly or unknowingly shamed someone? Have you ever experienced the fear of being stigmatised? Or discriminated against?

Stigma is generally associated with shame or dishonour. In simple words, it is a negative belief that a group of people or society has about something. In my experience of over three decades, whether it was in my earlier years of practice or in the present times, people still are concerned about the stigma attached to their difficulties or problems, especially in the mental health sector.

As soon as a child is suspected of having learning difficulties or is unable to sustain attention, and if he/she is referred to the therapist, parents begin to worry. They worry for many reasons. Their concerns are valid. They journey to and fro between denial and acceptance due to a variety of factors. A major concern is what our family will say. What will my friends say? Is he/she dumb? "Dumb?" Can we even use such a word? NO! The stigma attached to disability is brutal.

Awareness campaigns and awareness days are celebrated, but the stigma persists. How unfairly students with specific learning disabilities are treated in schools and the stigma that exists not only impacts academic abilities but also their emotional health?

When we understand what a specific learning disability is, we know that it does not include intellectual disability or learning problems caused by visual, hearing, or motor disabilities, environmental factors, or lack of English language proficiency. Of course, comorbidities might exist. Students' self-perception, self-efficacy, and mental health are negatively impacted more by the stigma surrounding learning disabilities (Agena et al., 2021).

When parents and teachers fail to recognise the stigma affecting students with specific learning disabilities, they will not be able to address and facilitate an inclusive environment.

Stigma is not just limited to specific learning disabilities; it could be associated with any illness, be it AIDS or Cancer. It could be a simple thing like delayed growth as per expected norms, and parents begin to shy away from society or build stories around their child's progress.

Ways You Can Reduce Stigma:

Talk openly about any ailment or mental health issue.

Educate yourself and others.

Be conscious of language. It is important to let people know that words matter.

Respect and treat people well. Do not judge or label them.

Do not let stigma cause you shame.

Seek help. Speak to a professional. If the professional shames or stigmatises you, report them to a professional organisation and consult a different professional.

> **"Mental illness is nothing to be ashamed of, but stigma and bias shame us all."**
>
> **– Bill Clinton**

Chapter Two

Use of Reversals

The most common sign when a child is suspected of having some difficulty in their academic work is the use of reversals and misspellings. My mantra is, "Catch them young. And remediate them immediately." Well, it didn't always work that way.

One such student was Lyla. Lyla was an adorable child. Full of mischief and fun. Lyla was eight when her mother came to me on an open day with her exam answer sheets. "Ma'am, I am telling you, she knew everything. She answered all the questions orally at home. She has even written everything on paper. But none of this makes sense. She is always making silly mistakes. She loses her marks for spelling…" Lyla's mother rattled on. There was a long queue of parents waiting to meet me. I looked at them; no way they were going to wait for me patiently. I took the bundle of papers from the helpless mother's hands and assured her that I would give her a patient hearing. And requested her to come and see me later that afternoon.

"Earlier, I heard you say she knew everything, but she makes silly mistakes…" I began. Well, I took the paper and showed it to her mother again. Pointing out every word and reading it quite fluently to her. She was amazed at what she heard and very confused at what she saw. I explained to her that Lyla had written the paper using all reversals. For us to understand, her 'w' had become 'm', 'y' turned to 'h', 'b' to 'd', and 'd' to 'b', and at times even 'u' became 'n'. At times, the word or the letter made sense. This is what her mother was unable to understand. "Why is 'bed' written correctly here but as 'deb' here?" She questioned. Her composition passage was well-expressed and meaningful. Sadly, it was full of spelling errors. It took at least an hour to introduce her to understand Lyla's difficulties.

Dear readers, are you able to read what Lyla has expressed here?

Working at a school that is inclusive but sets regulations to follow makes it tricky to manage the students within their academic timetable. Time slots were given to Lyla. Fortunately, Lyla was very sincere and she realised that something was amiss. We worked out a plan. A programme to follow at home was tailored too. Her mother was also involved, and she made it a point to follow up periodically.

We hadn't conducted a formal assessment yet. An informal assessment and therapy began. At this point, we found that she had poor concentration, her speed of reading was slow, she took longer to write, and copying from a green board was a task. Her mother did confess that she found it difficult to follow too many instructions if given together. She said Lyla had a good memory and was able to narrate a story of a movie in sequence, which she found quite intriguing.

It was understood that Lyla had visual processing challenges. She may have difficulties discriminating between images or their directionality, that is, which direction they face.

A year later, we did a formal assessment, and Lyla was diagnosed with dyslexia.

Dyslexia is a specific learning disability. It is characterised by difficulties in reading, writing, and spelling, and is caused by differences in the parts of the brain that process language (Davis & Braun, 1994). It is commonly associated with letter reversals. It is important to note that not all children with dyslexia use reversals.

If students have difficulty with directional knowledge, such as left-right and up-down, for example, b/d, p/q, h/y, n/u, and even in numbers like 6/9, 36/63, students will struggle with letter and number sequencing, leading to poor and inconsistent spelling, and difficulty in doing mathematics.

Lyla's mother mentioned that she loves to dance, but she noticed that Lyla made excuses during the dance lessons at school. Some of her classmates made fun of her because she was unable to follow instructions. But this was not as important to her at that moment as the importance given to academics in our society.

We took notice of this and immediately rescheduled her timetable. We did not allow her to skip her dance class. We worked with the dance teacher, and initially, we would put a red mark on her right hand like an 'r' that would remind her that it was her right hand.

Arrow exercises and p/b/d/q exercises were important parts of therapy. We encouraged her to play with a ball: catch it, bounce it, and squeeze it with soft balls. All of these were essential to improving hand-eye coordination, visual-spatial orientation, and fine motor and gross motor skills.

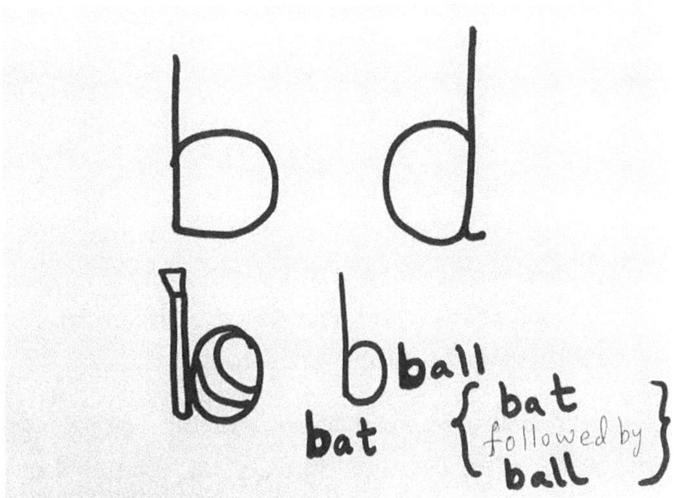

Part of the therapy included:

Use of colour for letter pairs. For example, initially, the letter b was always written in blue colour and the letter d in red. Even the printed book was highlighted until the errors became negligible. Audio cues were used for writing, e.g., for b, lo-bat ball (b is like the stick of bat first followed by a ball as shown in the image above).

Playing sorting and memory games was part of a fun schedule.

Practice visualising letters with closed eyes. Draw the shape in the air with your finger or use sensory materials like sand or clay to trace the letters.

Spotting the letters in various situations and places, like billboards, magazines, etc. Parents are encouraged to put up posters at home to reinforce the letters of the alphabet.

As we progressed, focus and attention shifted to reading and spelling difficulties. She benefited from a multi-sensory spelling programme, learning two to three words a day. Using visual pictures was helpful. She traced letters with her fingers (writing in sand or using cut-out letters to build words). The use of flashcards and matching games helped a lot.

For directionality, we used arrow exercises, games, and songs based on 'put your right hand in, put your right hand out...'; p-b-d-q exercises, mazes, and finger painting were also encouraged.

As she grew older, she learned to overcome her difficulties. The use of mnemonics was quite interesting as she came up with silly sentences (where the first letter of each word spells out the word you want to learn), which showed us her creative side. We taught her spelling rules later on, like how a 'q' is always followed by a 'u' and other simple rules.

Further, our next step was to group words and use different colours to highlight tricky parts of words. Writing words in different colours made learning quicker. For example: colour coding – education, vacation, application, and television, confusion, conclusion.

It was essential to celebrate small victories and accomplishments and focus less on correcting errors. The use of the colour red was discouraged in correcting errors. When there is too much red ink on a paper, the student feels more anxious and worries or has a fear of being reprimanded further.

Extra time was always considered for tasks that might take longer to complete. At the same time, she was encouraged to finish the task and compete to improve her time score.

Lyla scored very well in her 10th-grade board exams and her 12th-grade board exams too. It would be interesting to know that Lyla got into the commerce stream, graduated, completed her management studies, and is currently working abroad as an Associate Vice President in the banking sector.

do your best

{This story was previously discussed in our blog www. imperfect.co.in/decoding-dyslexia/}

Chapter Three

Self-Esteem

People often ask me an interesting question: What is a unique feature of what you do?

In many other professions, when a problem occurs, one follows a set of steps to troubleshoot and solve it. If an entire family catches the same stomach bug, the doctor will give them all the same medicine. Every time there is a specific problem on our website, our website team will run the same set of commands to solve the problem and get it up and running as before.

This is where therapy is vastly different and interesting. Therapy for each individual may differ even if the difficulty faced may be the same. The broader outline of the programme may be similar. Still, the varying individual needs individual environment, the conditions in which they live, the support system at home, the chronological age, and other comorbidities need to be considered while designing the specifics of an individual's remedial programme.

The biggest hassle one faces is the acceptance of the difficulty. There is always denial. There is often bargaining. "We, as parents, will work harder." "We have appointed special tuition." "We will make sure she does well in her exams." "He does well at home. It's only at school that he is performing poorly." These are just a few reasons that cause delays in beginning therapy. There is also the social stigma that plays an important role. Peer pressure is also critical. Peers should be buddies, and therapy should involve a buddy system to inculcate responsibility as well as acceptance or inclusion. An inclusive learning environment can benefit all students, not only those with disabilities. It helps students feel accepted and understood and boosts their confidence.

When a student is paired with another student to help them in school, they become buddies. A buddy system would work when a student needs social and emotional support. Students who need academic support would benefit when their buddies guide them in completing their notes or any schoolwork.

Students who underperform and struggle with their academic work, or those who have experienced repeated failures despite putting in effort, tend to have lower self-esteem. It is important to acknowledge their tiniest achievements and praise them for their effort and resilience.

Sunita was a quiet child with no eye contact, her fingers always turned in, and she was lost in her world, sitting quietly by herself. No one would notice her presence. "All she does is scribble in her books. She never completes her work and is daydreaming all day," her teacher complained. She added, "She never disturbs anybody; you will not even realise that Sunita is present in the classroom."

We had a meeting with Sunita's parents. Sunita's father was a busy man working in the police department. He did spend a few hours with Sunita during the week. Her mother, too, was busy with her corporate work and had little time to pay attention to Sunita's academic progress. They both thought that she was at school and was well taken care of. Her friend was their old maid who lived with them and looked after her. When at home, she would spend time watching television or staring out of the window. She had a tutor who came to her home to teach her.

Parents were requested to follow up after a month. We made a few changes to her daily schedule. We checked her books and the rough notebook. As the teacher had mentioned that she just scribbles, there was more to scribbling. She was talented. Her scribbles expressed a lot of emotions. We introduced her to an art class.

Working with Sunita was an interesting journey. Leading her parents towards acceptance was a more challenging part of it. They were convinced that nothing was wrong with Sunita, and they were absolutely right! However, they failed to understand that Sunita needed help and assistance to be noticed. Luckily, her parents were cooperative once they understood the difficulties Sunita was going through. Her mother managed to spend quality time with her adorable daughter. She was available for phone calls to discuss and manage schedules and programmes planned for Sunita. Her private tutor, too, was cooperative. She appreciated the efforts taken, learned a lot herself, and used innovative ways to teach concepts.

Important things that worked in therapy:

- Most important was to allow her to believe that she had the potential to achieve and reduce her fear of failing.

  - Creating a safe and supportive classroom environment.

- Involving classmates and giving them a sense of responsibility to assist Sunita only when needed.
- It was essential that her confidence be boosted, and there was no peer pressure.
- Teacher involvement was essential. They were requested to assign simpler tasks to her.
- Her art teacher played a vital role when she sent her drawing for a competition, and her work was selected. She has not won a prize yet; it was just the beginning. Her teacher encouraged her to participate in inter-school competitions, and she slowly gained recognition.
- Taking art as her strength, a lot of learning happened through doodles and visual cues.
- Positive reinforcement boosted her self-confidence and motivated her to strive for success.

It was understood that Sunita didn't have any learning difficulties, but she was never guided in the right direction. She was anxious about being in social situations and had difficulty expressing herself. Her lack of confidence further kept her away from interacting with others.

Because of her father's transferable job, Sunita had to leave school after a few years, but her mother kept in contact with me and updated me on Sunita's progress. Every 5th of September (celebrated as Teacher's Day in India), I definitely hear from Sunita. She continues her passion for art and always gives her friends and family original hand-painted items like scarves, napkins, bags, pillowcases, or cushions. She is now the loving mother of a two-year-old boy.

"I am capable, I am strong. I can, I will do my best."
"If I cannot do great things, I can do small things in
a great way."

– Martin Luther King

Chapter Four

Acceptance

Manisha was a cute, curly-headed bundle, full of energy. She would bang into things and injure herself ever so often. Her teacher came to me within a week of school reopening after the summer holidays. "This child needs help. I just don't seem to understand what she is writing. She holds her book in the most awkward position, and her head is almost touching the bench when she writes," she said. The next day, I glanced through her classroom. Manisha was sitting on the first bench, close to the blackboard. As mentioned by her teacher, her sitting posture was not usual. Her notebook was on the desk, drawn too close to her, and was almost touching her chest. She held the book tightly with her other hand, and her eyes strained as she raised her head to glance at the blackboard right in front of her. She was squinting her eyes as she tried to focus on the blackboard, attempting to find the word on it.

Manisha was from an economically challenged background. Her mother was a single parent who suffered from some ailment. She was preoccupied with problems of her own.

She was working hard to make ends meet. When I spoke to her, she was in total denial that something could be wrong with her daughter. It was only suggested that she meet up with an eye doctor. As the conversation progressed through patience, understanding, and empathy, she broke down and confessed that, due to financial constraints, she had overlooked this problem. A year back, eye surgery was suggested by a surgeon, but she had completely denied it, saying that she was fine and there was no need for surgery. We guided her mother to meet with another eye doctor for a second opinion. We arranged for sponsors to manage the cost of surgery. There was a lot of reluctance and hesitation. Finally, she was convinced after assurance from the doctor. Yes, there was risk involved, but without surgery, the risk of losing eyesight completely was greater.

Manisha returned to school after a month's break. She was able to see better than before, but she had to use corrective lenses. She could not handle being teased by classmates, and she would get really upset and resort to pinching or punching whoever teased her. She had anger issues and had difficulties with academics. The home environment was not enriching, and her mother also used to beat her when she was unable to manage her difficulties.

Fortunately for Manisha, she had a good set of friends who did indulge in teasing, but at the same time, they were very helpful. They would help her complete her notes, share their tiffin, and play with her. We also helped Manisha learn that when someone teases us about our appearance, it may not reflect something true about ourselves. In reality, it may be based on the teaser's own insecurity. We also helped her understand that children will join in to tease someone to avoid being teased themselves. This helped restore her self-esteem and feel better about herself, which automatically led to a decrease in what we previously saw as angry behaviour. This also helped the teachers and caretakers around her understand not to take behaviours at face value but to look underneath or behind the behaviour to identify and address its true cause effectively.

Manisha also had academic difficulties and could not cope with the regular school curriculum. She did not have any specific learning disabilities. According to the secondary state board, students with specific learning disabilities receive facilities and provisions such as extra time during examinations, the use of a scribe, or the option to choose vocational subjects instead of a second language. Without these facilities, her academic performance was on a downward trend. We arranged a meeting with the teachers concerned and her mother. It was decided that she would benefit from the Open School board curriculum.

Once again, her mother was in denial. Acceptance came with great difficulty. She had a meltdown. She almost fainted and was shocked to know that she would have to shift her daughter to another school. After satisfactory conversations and detailed discussions, the decision was taken to shift schools and move to a suitable board.

I must mention here that her mother was most dissatisfied. She even cursed the school system and maybe me, too, for making her take this step. I extended complete financial support to her and academic assistance after school hours. By now, Manisha was 14 years old, ready for grade ten. She had accepted that she would benefit from the Open School System.

Years went by, and one fine day, I saw this pretty girl standing at the door with an admirable smile. She had a small sweet box in her hand. She stretched it towards me and only said, "Thank you." My eyes watered, and I had the most serene smile on my face. After all, we did make the right decision.

Manisha had graduated with a degree in fashion and design. I bumped into Manisha two years ago. She proudly told me she supports her mother and is very happy now.

We don't always get to hear or see the end of stories we've been privileged to be a part of. But when we do, it reinforces our role, reminding us that our small, supportive role really matters. Of course, it feels good when parents recognise that we play an important role. But when a child can identify that our role was imperative in their well-being, although years later, it truly reminds us how important it is to stand up for those who may not have a voice, and how valuable it is to stand alongside them fiercely, even if we are the only two standing alone.

Chapter Five

Gratefulness

When you work in an institute with more than a thousand students, you deal with a variety of parents. There is a variety not only in culture and traditions but also in attitudes and nature. Some parents are ever so grateful. Some are so obliging, a few indulgent. Some never interfere or challenge the school system, while a set of parents are always whining or complaining.

Forum's mother is unique. Even as I type her story here, I feel overwhelmed. She is one mother who just doesn't stop showing me her gratitude.

I still remember her words when she met me for the first time. "Miss Tameh kai bhi karo. Ai chokri neh tameh kai samjavo." (Roughly translated as, Miss, do anything, but you please make this girl understand…). "Miss, please help me. I have tried everything, beating, punishing, and bribing, but she just can't read. I have to be with her all the time and read everything for her."

Forum was eight years old. She had an elder brother who also had difficulties in academics, but her mother described this difficulty as being a boy; he was playful and full of mischief. He could read and was managing his regular academic work.

Mother Rashi went on to tell me how she taught her. She gave me details of her daily schedule and the time spent on schoolwork done at home. There was no time for play. There was no time for Rashi to do any housework or her own practice as a beautician once Forum was home back from school.

She sounded so melodramatic at that time. She panted, she paused, and she shed a few tears. She would pause and look at me for approval on whether she should continue, or maybe she was checking if I was still listening to her. She was so desperate to seek help. She was young and pretty herself. Her hair was coloured at the roots. She was wearing a bit of makeup. I wondered when she got the time to colour her hair or wear makeup. She went on… However, her health was affected as she looked upon herself as a failure in managing her child.

We discussed Forum's reading and academic difficulties. We stressed the importance of understanding the root cause of the difficulty and how we could manage it. We also discussed in detail Forum's behaviour in different situations, including her attention span, hobbies, likes, and dislikes. Initially, we met Forum's mother every week to monitor and plan weekly programmes.

Rashi was very observant. She realised how her son too was facing difficulties and struggling, but she never noticed these as he was getting good grades at school. She confessed how impatient she was earlier and would scold Forum so often. She was a determined mother and accepted that her children had specific learning disabilities. Rashi put a lot of effort into both her kids and encouraged them to study.

Whenever we meet, she makes it a point to say thank you. If either of us is with friends and we see each other, she will make it a point to tell them how her eyes were opened and how "I" became her saviour. It was only because of me that her daughter studied until the twelfth grade.

I give full credit to Rashi for being so cooperative and having faith in me. I am ever so grateful to Rashi and Forum for their confidence in me.

Part of the therapy programme involved:

Use of mnemonics—Different methods were used: the peg word method, acronyms, and the keyword method. These techniques were used to spell difficult words, memorise information, and recall information learned.

Exercise was an important part of the programme as we had to increase her attention span.

Music played in the background while studying helped her focus and stay calm.

The program was planned with achievable short-term goals.

Focusing on one concept at a time.

Frequent breaks between tasks.

Positive motivation.

Playing memory games.

This story brings up the subtle and often overlooked difference in how we view the behaviour of boys and girls differently. Many behaviours, when seen in females, are seen more easily as problematic. The same behaviour in males is seen more easily as an attribute of being a 'boy'. I write about this not just to highlight this difference in our perception. This difference also leads to a delay in addressing concerns that male children face. That delay can have major consequences.

Reflection for readers:

Dear readers, have you noticed someone like Forum or her brother? How do you think things will be for Forum as she grows up? What would you do if you came across someone showing signs of difficulties in reading? Spend some time reflecting on whether you would wait longer to flag these difficulties for a boy or a girl. And why?

CHAPTER SIX

Reading – A Mystery

"Why do I have to read? Can't I just look at the pictures and understand the story? Please tell me the story, I promise I will listen with attention. This reading is like a mystery to me, like this story!" blurted Fiona when we began with a simple, colourful reader.

Mystery is something that you cannot understand or explain. I agree with Fiona; reading is a mystery.

Fiona was unique. She was imaginative and, I would say, a good guesser. She would guess the words she read but was very inconsistent.

Well, that's what we call dyslexia, isn't it? There were issues not only with reading but with information processing, memory, and organisational skills.

We started from scratch. Luckily, alphabet recognition and sounds were achieved. We began with three-letter words and a phonic base and progressed to blends. Here, we used flashcards and played 'match the word to the picture' games. Blends were introduced, and we combined them with word endings. For example, bl + end = blend, tr + end = trend. Word groups were introduced one at a time to avoid confusion in the minds of our young students. For example, bl + and = bland...

An Individualised Educational Programme was planned.

An IEP or an Individualised Educational Programme is a written programme for an individual that is planned, implemented, and reviewed as per the needs of the individual (Price-Ellingstad et al., 2000).

The involvement of parents was necessary to follow up at home. We helped the parents with ideas on adapting the activities we would practice in sessions to using materials easily available at home. For example, pick a page from a magazine or newspaper for word recognition, mark a particular area with a marker, and ask the child to find the words from the marked area. Or highlight a known word and ask the child to find the same word on paper or in a magazine. Similarly, find the same sounding words, synonyms, antonyms, and so on.

It is probable that the story of the three wise men visiting infant Jesus was woven around this astronomical phenomenon. However, the New Testament states the *Magi* were astronomers and astrologers who saw a special star, followed it and found the child (son of God), and presented him with gold, frankincense and myrrh. Early Christians saw significance in each: gold for the King, frankincense for divinity and myrrh for human nature.

The method used to remediate was to engage all the senses such as sight, sound, and touch. We used a sandbox. We also used thicker pens or markers to trace the words with our fingers. The child was encouraged to say the word out loud and trace the word at the same time.

> **Sacred Trees**
>
> In England, there are many sacred old trees. The individual spirits of trees were worshipped by the Druid priests of ancient Europe. Trees were regarded by these ancients as 'residence of the earth spirit.' They also believed that the earth spirit finds its receptacle / residence in springs, wells, rivers, rocks and caverns.

The programme aimed to teach phonics, decoding, and comprehension skills. She was encouraged to read aloud, which could improve her decoding skills and reading comprehension. Repeated reading experiences and multiple exposures to words were provided. She was encouraged to recognise words in different places or situations while travelling on buses, in advertisement hoardings, and from magazines or newspapers.

Peer support was required and easily established as she was a friendly child with a caring attitude. All her classmates were ready to help. Her friends were assigned duties to assist her in different subjects.

Positive feedback to encourage her and build her self-esteem was essential.

Fiona can read now. She is a mother to a cute baby boy. Influenced by her mother, she enjoyed doing makeup and became a beautician specialising in hair styling and facials.

Did you find Fiona's story familiar? Perhaps you've read it before on our blog: *https://imperfect.co.in/dyslexia-therapy-young-readers/*

Reading was not only a mystery to Fiona but to many other students too. Ashtad, too, struggled with reading. But with therapy, guidance, and support, he managed to read. He was energetic and affectionate. He was attending a boarding school.

I also had the opportunity to work with a few kids who were boarders. These kids are really special to me, as I truly admire them. They not only attend their academic school but also prepare themselves for their priesthood. These young boys have a strictly disciplined life. According to the Zoroastrian religion, these boys who prepare for the priesthood need to know their prayers, understand the rituals, and be able to perform them once they are ordained as priests.

They, too, face difficulties with their academics and need guidance and support. Depending on their individual needs, therapy was planned. Despite their tightly packed schedule, they would eagerly attend remedial sessions. I truly appreciated their dedication and commitment. Difficulties were related to the English language, either with reading, writing, spelling, mathematics, or all of them. With the provisions provided by the State Board of Maharashtra, the students get a valid certificate after going through the assessment process. This entitles the students to the provisions for their examinations. With these benefits, most of them do well in their grade ten board examinations.

Reflections for readers:

Dear readers, do you know which other states in India provide provisions for students with specific learning disabilities?

Do you think students who receive these provisions use them confidently? Can you think of a few reasons why they may shy away from using them, even though they require them?

CHAPTER SEVEN

Numbers in Space

To be honest, I have never had the opportunity to work with this intelligent girl. She was focused. She did well academically for her age. She was 14, a determined teenager, very good at sports, and actively involved in organising school events.

This was three decades ago. I was newly appointed. There were no provisions at the SSC board level. Dyslexia was still making its way into the mainstream. I had little practical experience in dealing with teenage tantrums. Her mother approached our dear principal, and she spoke to her at length. I was called in for a meeting. Her mother, father, our principal, the bold teenager, and I. We sat around the table. I was informed that Kai was failing miserably in mathematics. But she was brilliant in other academic subjects. She was scoring less in physics, too.

I had a short conversation with her. "All I see are numbers in space," she said. We discussed many options and tried counselling and tricks to manage this difficulty in mathematics.

Finally, I was told that a decision had been made. Kai left school, and I believe she did her 10th-grade examination through the Open School System. She graduated in the field of humanities. Being a creative person and with her love for art, she is an Independent Creative Professional.

CHAPTER EIGHT

Second Childhood

I grew up living in a joint family system. I got married, and we chose to live as a joint family. As my in-laws got older, the need to look after them changed. My understanding as a caregiver was limited then, but as we know, old age is like your second childhood, and soon I understood how to manage it. Early signs of Alzheimer's set in with my mother-in-law. I did some online courses to understand how to manage the situation. Initially, I was excited and made worksheets to keep her mind occupied. It was important to try to take control of the deteriorating memory.

I go for my daily walks to a nearby garden. Many senior citizens visit this park. It occurred to me, why not assist our seniors, too?

This was the beginning of the Mental Health Enrichment Programme that I founded, intending to promote social, emotional, intellectual, and physical development, facilitate and impart knowledge, build confidence, and critical and analytical thinking skills, and make an individual self-sufficient. An age limit of 60+ years was set.

A programme was developed to reinforce the skills required through a system of cognitive exercises that enhance the ability to distinguish, process, and retain information to enhance a healthy mind and body. The programme involved the use of simple techniques and exercises, learning through fun, focusing on breathing, group talks, and sharing.

This group of seniors was the most affectionate lot. They were full of energy and wisdom. Every Monday, messages on our WhatsApp group went click, click, "Is there class today? Koun aveche?" (roughly translated to "Who is attending the class today?") Our fortnightly programme was eagerly awaited by this group of very enthusiastic, inspiring young people. This is the group for whom I waited to meet fortnightly, and I would never want to miss seeing them.

They were insightful, caring, and eager to learn. You would be surprised to know how most of them adapted to technology at such a young age and attended these programmes even online all through the pandemic. As you would expect, there was a lot of "Can you hear me?" "Can you see me?" and "Your voice is breaking, can you repeat, please?" But the wonders of neuroplasticity made this a successful mode of meeting despite the odds.

What we did in our gatherings:

Activities to stimulate and maintain cognitive skills.

Use arts and crafts, various hobbies, yoga, and gentle exercises.

Focus on breathing.

Brain gym and more.

Physically stimulating activities.

Activities such as music, dance, puzzles, quizzes, and housie for shared social interaction.

Group discussions, talks, and sharing on various topics.

Special occasions and celebrations.

But these were just a few I personally interacted with. They may have their own stories to tell and mechanisms to cope. They looked forward to attending these sessions, and it was an opportunity for them to communicate with others.

Many older individuals are not fortunate enough to socialise in any form. Social isolation is one of the most common problems affecting seniors, and we can't ignore its effects. As they retire, or due to health concerns, they tend to spend more time at home and limit themselves from getting out into the community and spending time with others.

To stay in good mental and physical health, social interaction is very important. Social isolation is associated with cognitive decline, poor memory, and even higher mortality rates in older adults. Our seniors must spend enough quality time with friends, family, or other members of the community.

What are the things that one could do to help our seniors avoid social isolation?

Visit

Generally, seniors do not get out of their house either due to ill health or fear of falling. So, if you know of any senior person living in your society, building, or home, check with them if they would like some company. Talk to them. If they are confident, take them out for a walk or to the park.

Visit a park, and if you see any seniors by themselves, interact with them.

Social meals

Mealtime is an innately social activity, so regularly eating alone can increase feelings of loneliness. It is one of the times when seniors feel the most social isolation.

Try to visit your parents or grandparents during mealtime. Meet up with their friends, gather their friends together, and arrange for senior get-togethers during mealtimes.

Phone chats/Video chats

If you or your senior loved one lives far from friends and family, use video chat to stay in regular contact.

Transport

Drive them to a place they may want to visit, help them book a cab, find a taxi for them, and, if possible, accompany them on an outing.

How can seniors help themselves (Donohue, 2020)?

Meal time

Eat with others as often as you can. This may reduce feelings of isolation. Invite guests over for a meal and occasionally dine at a restaurant.

Neighbours

Interacting with our neighbours allows them to get to know us. This helps them know that we may need to reach out to them, and it is comforting for us to know that support is available.

Visit a park

Call a friend, meet them at the park, take a walk, and try to stay active. There are many parks where there are laughter clubs or people who exercise together, practice breathing, or do yoga. Join them, and do your bit.

In-home care

If you live alone, hiring a caretaker at home allows you to receive help with chores and promotes daily interaction with another human being. With their assistance, you may also be better able to visit other places of interest and remain connected to the larger community.

Adapt to technology

Seek help from the younger generation, learn technology, and stay occupied.

Hearing and vision care

Do not ignore hearing aids. If you can hear well, you may stay alert and engaged in the present moment. Also, regularly get your vision checked.

Seek help

A counsellor or a therapist will listen to you without judgment and may assist you in addressing the causes and solutions to interact with others. They may guide you in finding or reaching out to family, friends, or your community. The pandemic has led to an increase in the availability of online therapy and support. Most professionals continue to function online, too.

Try to help your elderly loved one by finding more opportunities for them to interact with others, ensuring they're in good health, and getting the most out of life.

Reflections for the reader:

Did you know? The brain changes associated with cognitive decline actually begin during our 20s! So, if you were thinking, "This isn't a problem I need to deal with for years to come," you might need to reconsider.

Chapter Nine

Our Language – Our Words Matter

Amidst the daily hustle and bustle of our lives, we fail to use our words carefully.

There is no reason to shout, yell, get angry, or be annoyed at the slightest of things, but we often do so. We all would like to be addressed with respect and spoken to politely, but we don't consciously do the same to others. Well, I wish we could all make an effort.

In my experience of working with children, adults, and families, special needs or not, I learned to be patient. Patience was my strong point. But with age and hormonal changes, patience was running out...

I often hear teachers in the classroom using inappropriate words. They surely don't mean what they say, but it is that instant, that moment, that one has to be most careful about.

My training in narrative therapy helped me to stay calm and non-judgmental. It certainly plays an important role in my life as a mental health professional.

This data has been collected about the awful language one tends to use in 'those' moments with the help of some students, a few parents, and colleagues.

There are other factors to consider, too, like tone, posture, and attitude. If we would only take a moment before we blurt out, and try to take a deep breath before the words pour out, we would surely touch more hearts.

With the help of the table below, we could attempt to mind our language.

At school:

Inappropriate Language	Appropriate Language
You don't know how to behave in class – stupid!	Your behaviour tells me you are having trouble with something. Can you tell me if you need help?
Useless, dumb girl. You moron.	From your question, I understand that you have not understood this topic. Would you like me to explain this again?
Get out of my class. I should take you to the principal. You are disturbing everybody.	This disruptive behaviour is not expected in the classroom. Can we leave it outside? It would be appreciated if you feel restless, can we discuss some ideas you can ponder on when you step out and return when the feeling has settled?

Inappropriate Language	Appropriate Language
Use your brains!	How about giving some thought to what is being discussed? Let's apply our knowledge. Let's think about the situation. Let's think about the concept. Can we think about this again?
Don't act like a spastic.	I understand it is difficult to sit on these hard benches. Can we quietly get up, stretch our legs and arms, and get back to our routine?
Stop fidgeting and pay attention.	Is it possible to clear our desk and push everything inside the desk?
Daydreamer! / Sleeping Beauty!	This is not a very interesting topic for some, but we can't afford to skip it. It is an important topic, so if we could try to focus a bit here, please.
(When a child is looking out of the window) Is there a flying pony outside your window?	I understand there are more important things happening around us, but it would be valued if we could listen to what is being said here.
No badge? No belt? Look at your hair! Now you come naked to school.	It seems we didn't have enough time to dress up completely. Would you like to take a few minutes to straighten things out?

Inappropriate Language	Appropriate Language
You are such a crybaby! Stay at home if you can't adjust here.	It seems that something is troubling you (or bothering you). I am here if you wish to speak to me. If you prefer not to share it with me, I can arrange for you to go over to the counsellor's cabin to have a word.
Get used to it and toughen up.	This change in the new environment is making you upset. Would you like to talk about it?
Who will marry you? You are so irresponsible. You can't do a simple thing!	Is it okay for you to try to complete the task assigned to you? Do you need any assistance with this task? Would it be of interest to you if you could take up this task responsibly?

At home:

Inappropriate Language	Appropriate Language
Are you mad?	I understand this incident is troubling you. Do you want to have some time to yourself?
I wish you were never born!	This behaviour is unacceptable. Do you need some help to sort things out?

Inappropriate Language	Appropriate Language
Who will ever love you?	As your parent or sibling, I see that you are seeking attention in inappropriate ways. Would you like to share your feelings?
You are worthless.	I have observed that you are unable to make correct decisions. I understand that it is difficult for you to make a choice. Would you like some help?
You can never do anything right.	If this job that you just finished or this decision that you have made does not seem favourable, would you like to reconsider it?

We know our words have power. They can affect people in many ways:

Emotionally, physically, and intellectually.

They influence our thoughts, beliefs, and actions.

They may boost or lower our self-confidence and well-being.

They may weaken or strengthen our relationships.

They may discourage or encourage us to fulfil our goals.

People judge us by our words.

Let us be inspiring and encouraging.

> *As the Lord says, "The soothing tongue is a tree of life,*
> *but a perverse tongue crushes the spirit."*

Reflections for the reader:

Let's take some time to reflect on a time when we may have used words or a tone that we didn't really want to. Why did we say that? Do we even know what it means? Did we even want to say those words?

Doubtful…

Then why did we say it?

We often say things we have heard others say frequently. Have you heard a young child tell their younger sibling, "Stop eating my head?" They surely do not mean that, right? They simply repeat what was said to them.

This is a similar but simply put explanation of how generational trauma also cascades and gets propagated. How do we stop this complex chain of events? Can we stop it all at once? How do we even begin?

Perhaps we can start by deciding that,

It stops with us!

And then we take a moment to think before we respond.

Oh, and between one and two, there will be tons and tons of self-work, introspection, processing, growth, etc., done in a variety of ways, perhaps with the help of some therapy.

Sounds extremely effortful and complex, doesn't it? It truly is!

Then why do it? Can you imagine a world where we don't use words in the left half of the above table at all? Can you imagine what would happen if we comfort little children while they cry instead of telling them to be strong or to shut up?

A world where kids learn to listen to themselves, value their feelings and emotions, and learn how to regulate what they feel, think critically and are given the power to challenge what they hear. A world of well-adjusted people. Wouldn't all that effort be worth it then?

This reminds me of a dialogue between Winnie the Pooh and Piglet: "Some people talk to animals. Not many listen, though. That's the problem," said Pooh.

And this one too,

"It makes such a difference to have someone who believes in you," said Pooh.

Chapter Ten

Dealing with Trauma

(Trigger warning: death by suicide, trauma)

Kajal, a student in grade four, was very vocal and expressive. She had sparkling eyes and a voice that was most pleasant to the ear. Kajal excused herself from her classroom, seeking permission to visit the washroom. Story of all the teachers, "Ma'am, may I go to the toilet? It's coming fast! Please, ma'am." Kajal was granted permission; little did the teacher know that she had come to visit me. I sometimes wondered whether I should immediately report this matter to the teacher concerned. Here, I chose to listen to Kajal. She honestly told me that she excused herself to visit the washroom but wanted to speak to me.

I thought she could have waited until break time to seek an appointment. It was as if she were reading my mind. "This is urgent, and there will be too many people around during break time. I don't want my friends to know I am here," she blurted.

Go on, I signalled. "Last evening around seven o'clock, Mom went to the market. She had given me some work to complete in my homework book. I heard a loud THUD. At first, I thought it was nothing, but still, I went to the balcony to see what the sound was about. I peeped through our railing and saw blood splashed all around. A man was lying there on the ground. I was so scared. I just could not say anything. I was shaking and crying. When I peeked again, the security uncle was running and calling people. Luckily, my mom came home in a few minutes, and I cried. She held me tight. I felt better, but I could not sleep all night. I am very scared. Why did that uncle jump?" She gave me details, describing things that happened, and I was able to visualise the entire scene like a Hindi movie. In between, there were breaks, sobs, fear in those shiny eyes, and cold, sweaty hands. Kajal added. "Mom has no answers. Papa is also saying to try to forget what I saw. He said that the uncle had some difficulty; he may have lost his balance."

I let her know that it was unfortunate that she had to witness this situation, that she was a brave girl, and that she made the right decision to come see me. This was an emergency. We discussed what she expected from me. I had to remind myself that she was just a nine-year-old. She was nervous, scared, and sought help. I went with the flow, listening to her patiently. In between, I sent a handwritten note to her teacher informing her that she was with me since she would worry about why Kajal was taking so long in the washroom.

We discussed, we spoke, and she led me to talk about life, its importance, and whether she could have done anything to help this uncle. I sat there wondering how these little minds work, how this little girl thinks. We cracked a joke later, and slowly she felt a bit calm. She said she was ready to go back to class. I requested her to visit me at any time of the day if she felt uncomfortable and asked her to definitely see me before going home. I also let her know that with her permission if she feels so, we could meet up with her parents too.

The school bell rang for prayers, and it was time to go home. Kajal was at the door. She smiled, showed me a thumbs-up, and left. I was relieved, but it was hard to believe that the child who went through so much was fine.

The next morning, I was called into the school office. Kajal's mother was there. She wanted to meet me. "Kajal is sobbing and refuses to come to school," she said to me. "She mentions your name and says, 'I can't go to school.'" I was stunned! Thoughts raced through my mind. Did she make up the whole story? Was I fooled? Am I so stupid? I took a deep breath and asked Kajal's mother if we could talk for some time.

In our session, I realised my thoughts were useless. Kajal did go through the trauma, and her parents were not able to answer her questions. But why did she not want to see me?

We learned that the entire morning when she was with me, she had missed a lot of work in the classroom and could not tell her mother why. It seems that Kajal, our very verbal kid, did not like to write, and she was shouted at for coming home again with incomplete work.

We spoke at length and discussed how we as a team could assist Kajal in dealing with this situation. Luckily, I had her prior permission to speak with her parents, as maintaining confidentiality is important in therapy sessions.

It was decided that Kajal would meet me for a few sessions until she was confident, and whatever work she missed in the classroom would be written by her peers. Her mother was permitted to complete her notes for a short period.

I myself was a novice in dealing with trauma for the client. It was made clear to the parents that they could seek help from outside if needed. I discussed with my mentors and supervisors how to manage and handle this aspect of therapy. We even had a demo session among us before I could start therapy with Kajal. It was such a wonderful learning experience.

Kajal settled quite well, and her parents also learned not to pressure her with her academics.

Here, I would like to mention things that one should keep in mind about a few mistakes therapists should be mindful of:

It is very important to maintain confidentiality. To violate confidentiality would be a big mistake.

Rapport building is essential to reaching out to clients. The client-therapist bond enhances therapy and motivates the client to work with the therapist to fulfil therapy goals.

The therapist should be honest, and if the therapy is outside his/her purview, he/she should inform the client and guide the client to the appropriate therapist.

Therapists should be empathetic and excellent listeners.

Reflections for the reader:

Before reading this story, did you presume that kids aren't capable of thinking about existential topics of life, existence, death, meaning, etc.?

Why is it so hard for adults to imagine that kids can think deeply?

Can you think about a time when a young person asked you a deep question and you brushed it off because you assumed they wouldn't understand the answer or even the question they had asked?

How could you have responded while valuing their question and intellect, but in an age-appropriate way?

CHAPTER ELEVEN

Writing – How Do I Write without Making Mistakes?

Two years after Kajal's incident, there was a phone call from Mrs. Shah. The name popped up on my phone in the missed call list. There was a WhatsApp message seeking an appointment to discuss the difficulties Kajal is facing. Once again, the mind was as delicate as it could be, and thoughts raced through once more. But this time, I pushed them aside and gave the parents a suitable time for our meeting.

Kajal's mother, Mrs. Shah, arrived on time. She was draped in a sari with a typical bandhani red-green print. She came alone with just a notebook—Kajal's tuition notebook. Red marks were visible everywhere, with remarks like "work hard!", "Not studying!", "Please learn again!" and "Write 10 times" were grossly visible. Spellings were underlined, sometimes twice, and in some places thrice, with many encircled. It looked like a book dipped in red ink. The book said it all. Her mother observed me intensely as I went through the pages, pausing and tracing my finger over certain words. I closed the book and looked at her. Her face was like that of a curious child who had no clue what was happening around her.

We discussed her daily schedule, study schedule, who teaches her at home, etc. Her mother expressed that she is very good orally and has a good memory, too. But still, she makes errors while writing and refuses to write. After coaxing, when she starts to write, she will want breaks or complain of aches and pains. She added that her school notebooks are often incomplete.

We did an informal assessment. It was suggested that we get an evaluation done by an occupational therapist. We had to work with an occupational therapist to help. The informal assessment revealed signs of specific learning difficulties. A programme was planned.

We need to understand that some children may write more slowly than others. It is not just because they cannot write faster; they may also take longer to process the information. They need breaks, too, as pain or tiredness may be due to the grip or pressure used to hold a pencil or a pen. Handwriting requires fine motor skills.

Therapy included:

She was introduced to using a pencil gripper. The gripper helped her hold the pencil firmly and guided the amount of pressure required while writing on paper.

Occupational therapy helped improve hand strength, fine motor coordination, and correct body posture for writing.

Positive self-talk to manage writing difficulties.

For spellings,

Games like the alphabet mat involve placing letters on chart paper and rolling a dice. Depending on the length of the words (3/4/5/6 letters), players pick the letters where the dice lands and form words, which can be phonetic words or sight words.

Word sequencing games in alphabetical order.

Building blend words (provide a set of blends, e.g., Br, gr, bl, pl, and other sets like...ock, ick, ay, etc.)

Worksheets based on spell check.

Word-building games.

Spot the word.

Grow the sentence.

Word ladders.

Write the missing part of the words. (e.g. Appli—----cation/ multi—----cation...)

Colour coding, boxing, and grouping words were used to teach spelling.

Highlighting words in text.

Certain spelling rules were taught, like the letter 'q' is always followed by 'u'.

Or

To teach a bunch of '**ie**' words for the "i before e" rule, e.g., believe, relieve, grieve, achieve. Let them know the rule, sing it, tune it. "i before e, when the sound is eee, except after the letter c, we use ei. E.g., receive, ceiling, receipt."

Teach the exceptions later. E.g., weigh, neighbour, sleigh (the sound is 'ai').

Use different coloured pens, pencils, or markers, and index cards. Write the words boldly. Make a mental picture of that card, read the word aloud, spell it aloud, and change how you say the 'hard part', maybe saying it louder or putting on an accent. So, you'd write: separate. When you write the whole word, think about the hard part, what it looks like or sounds like. So, while you're writing 'separate', you might be thinking 'sep-AY-rate'.

For writing, cloze procedure passages were used.

Exercise to work on spatial orientation: Arrow exercise. P, B, D, Q exercise.

A multi-sensory approach was essential.

Depending on one's needs, the following modifications may be helpful:

Writing assignments could be short.

Assignments with spelling errors or punctuation mistakes should be accepted and corrected later.

Extra time should be allocated to complete classwork or homework.

May be allowed to use computers to write tests.

Make use of assistive technology. Use tools such as text-to-speech software, digital intervention programmes, or specialised reading apps.

Make the classroom supportive.

Make the home environment encouraging and engaging.

CHAPTER TWELVE

Is it ADHD? A Case Study

This chapter is about a session with Anil, a ten-year-old who used to get into trouble at school and was unable to focus in the classroom.

In our sessions, we used narrative therapy to understand our problem and work towards resolving it.

The initial session was spent building rapport between the therapist and Anil. Anil had learned that to gain sympathy from a teacher, he needed to make them feel bad. He did that by introducing a very sad story that involved his 'bad friend' and himself, where his bad friend met with an accident because he did mean things to him. This story was narrated to me to judge me. We talked about the things that we would be discussing together. I explained to him the concept of confidentiality, and the stories unfolded. We moved on to rich story development.

What was amazing was the way he was able to come up with wonderful illustrations and his ideas and thoughts to work on every aspect that was interfering with his daily work.

Some of the questions asked during our session and the responses are noted:

Therapist: Would you like to describe your school day to me?
Anil: I play, I eat, and I sit on a bench. {Anil}
T: If I were a fly in your classroom, what would I see you doing?
A: Looking at the teacher.

T: What tactics does "the focus going away thing" use?

A: Throwing rubber bands at children.

T: How does "the focus going away" try to set itself up?

A: Some songs come to mind. Feel very sleepy

T: Do you think "the focus going away" has a way of making its impact felt?

A: The teacher will make me sit on a bench during break time.

T: What are your thoughts on what is going on here?

A: I should try to pay attention.

T: Would you be able to tell me a bit about what "the focus going away" is doing here?

A: Bringing in other thoughts. If I pay attention, I will get good marks in the assessment.

T: When you have just said what is important to you, what ideas do you have about any new steps you could take?

A: I should work hard. I should sleep early.

T: Do you get any mental pictures or images of how you would like "the focus to come back"?

A: He came up with this wonderful illustration to regain his focus.

He used this strategy in his classroom quite often and was thrilled that he could regain his focus on his own.

Later, his concern was how to keep the focus and not lose it.

We had a wonderful "remembering conversation". Here, he thought of Mahabharata, where King Dhritarashtra was the leader of soldiers. He described how he would protect his soldiers and how the soldiers would use the shields; similarly, he came up with an illustration, too.

A soldier with 20 shields surrounds his ears, protecting him and stopping the outside noises that keep disturbing him. The shields would be able to protect him from outside noises, allowing him to concentrate, and he would be able to study well. He thought his parents and grandparents would feel very happy and proud of him, too.

He was thrilled that at school, he could not hear any other noises; he could hear only the "noises of lessons." He was able to focus his attention, and he heard his teacher say, "Anil, you are becoming a good boy." He was able to ask his teacher the meanings of words, too. He had made some friends, as they, too, thought that he was not very naughty anymore.

He wanted to be excellent, but his concern was "the irritating voice". Our sessions continued. He came up with a Captain America shield (which is the strongest shield in the world). He said he would use this shield so the irritating voice would disappear. He wanted to study, be intelligent, and have more friends. Anil was really happy with how he used his techniques in school or while studying, and he felt proud that people were telling him that he was becoming a good boy. He saw himself in the future as not being rude, not being mean, and sharing his things with everyone. He would be working hard and being helpful.

Reflections for the reader:

Can you predict what a well-equipped path we have set Anil up for in dealing with his future difficulties? Could you notice the role of the agency we gave Anil in coming up with strategies that worked for him and ones he was able to imagine and execute himself?

Spend some time reflecting on how ineffective it may have been to just tell him to "pay attention."

CHAPTER THIRTEEN

An Insight Into a Group Session with the Use of Narrative Therapy

A group of five students from grade five was referred to me. The teacher mentioned that they were struggling with their daily work, but they did fine during their tests and assessments.

It was observed that there was a kind of stigma attached to seeing a counsellor or visiting the resource room. But they had to meet me, so they came to me with long faces, most disheartened and unwilling. (Note: K = therapist; students, S1, S2, S3, S4, S5 = students one, two, three, four, and five)

K: Hello, good morning.

S: Good morning, ma'am.

K: Hey, tell me, what's it like for all of you to come to see me?

S: Our mistress told us to see you.

K: Well, it would be helpful for me to know what Miss wants me to know about.

S1: As we don't complete our work, she always shouts at and punishes us.

K: What are your concerns?

S3: We don't want to come here; our friends will not talk to us, they will tease us, not play with us, and tell everybody.

K: Is this the first time you've put words to what you are worried about?

S: Well, yes, but...

K: I hear you say that your concerns are what your friends will think and that they will not play with you.

S2: Yeah, but this is what I think, and she thinks too.

K: So, if I were a little butterfly in the school playground, what would I see you all do during break time?

S1: Play with friends.

S2: Eat.

S3+S4: Play and eat.

S5: I like to sit and watch, sometimes I play.

K: Could you tell me a bit more about playing with friends?

No response; they shrug and look at each other.

K: You say you are worried that your friends will not play, would you like to give a name to this?

S: Means? Name?

K: This feeling that friends will not talk, what does it look like? What would you like to call it?

S1: Worried to come here.

S4: Friends worry.

S2: Worry. Scared.

S5: Friend Problem.

K: Do I hear you say, 'The friend problem'?

I must confess here that it was difficult to manage talking to five in a group and framing questions. It was a task. However, I gathered that they were enjoying being in a group and were eager to answer the questions.

K: What, in particular, did you notice 'the friend problem' doing?

S4: Nothing, they will think we are weak, we are dumb.

K: What does 'being dumb' mean to you?

S1: Not studying.

S2: Not completing work.

S3: Getting remarks.

K: When I see you not completing work, who would help you finish it?

S: My friend will help me.

S2: Our friends are nice; they help us.

K: How does 'the friend problem' affect you on a day-to-day basis?

S1: It does not affect us; I am worried they will not talk.

S2: I think they will think I am weak in my studies.

K: Does the name 'the friend problem' that you all have decided for this issue still fit, or do you have any other thoughts? What would you call it?

S: Worry problem!

S2: We are worried. We will not have any friends.

K: How does 'the worry problem' affect you on a day-to-day basis?

S3: I worry about completing homework.

S2: I don't like to write.

S4: I just worry at school because I don't complete my work.

S: Our teacher dictates very quickly.

K: What would the teacher experience when this worry problem is in full force?

Stares!

K: What would the teacher notice when this worry is in full force?

S2: I will tell her I am not well; my head is hurting.

S1: My partner will write for me, or I will take her book. The teacher will not say anything. She knows I can't write fast.

S3 + S4: We will also copy it later.

K: What are your thoughts on what's going on here?

S: We should write quickly.

S5: We should pay attention. We should not talk.

K: So, what are you saying is more important right now?

S: We must pay attention, not talk.

S2: And write quickly.

K: Now that I hear you say, to pay attention, not talk in class when the teacher is around, and write fast, what ideas do you have about any steps you could take?

S: We will not worry.

K: Can you say a bit more about why you are taking this position?

S: Our friends help us.

S4: They are nice.

K: What are you saying is important to you right now?

S: We must work hard.

K: Do you have any thoughts or ideas? What ideas do you have about any step you could take?

S5: Hmmm! Can you help us?

S3: We can come to you. Can we?

S: We must study daily. If we don't understand, we will ask the teacher.

S2+S4: Yes, yes, we must come to you. We like talking to you.

S: Thank you for talking to us :)

This was one of the most amazing group sessions I had with a group of kids.

CHAPTER FOURTEEN

Language Barrier

In an English-medium school generally, everyone speaks the English language, at least to the teachers, and the curriculum is taught in English. Of course, at times, students communicate with each other in their mother tongue.

Have you experienced Mumbai rains? I am sure most of you have. Dark clouds make the day gloomy. Roads get flooded, and there is chaos. At school, we anticipate and dread the announcement that students may be allowed to go home if parents come to collect their wards. Parents living in the nearby areas, where waterlogging is prevalent, wade their way through the waters and come to pick up their children.

One such rainy day, when we anticipated a holiday in Mumbai due to heavy downpours, I was called to the principal's office. Mr. Gupta sat tall in a checked brown shirt, full sleeves, and smart trousers. He appeared to me like an inspector from the educational office. My principal signalled me to take a seat. She introduced me to Mr. Gupta and his daughter, Rima, whom I noticed only

when she pointed at her. Rima was wearing a pretty pink frilly dress, with lots of oil in her hair as though the entire bottle of oil was settled there. Her hair was styled tightly in two pigtails. She sat in the corner of the room with a doll and was stacking some books in the office. She told me, "Mr. Gupta was seeking admission for Rima. Mr. Gupta added, "Hamare ghar ke koi bhi bachhe, angreji medium mein nahi padhe hai. Hum chahte hain ki hamari bitiya angreji school mein padhe." (None of the kids in my family have studied in English. I wish that my daughter could study in an English medium.) I am certain that at that moment my mouth was left wide open, wide enough for even a rat to enter. "Well, what do you think, Kashmira? Should we consider granting admission to Rima?" She asked me for my opinion. I glanced at her, and she signalled me to chat with Rima. I moved towards the adorable Rima. She had the cutest smile, and she was talking to her doll. I thought she was acting like a teacher and teaching something to her doll. I didn't catch her words, but it did seem so at that moment. We chatted for a while, I picked up a piece of paper and gave her some colours, we drew some things, and she coloured neatly. And we built rapport. She was a smart learner. We understood each other. We were able to communicate.

"Well?" I was asked again. "Ma'am, we can give it a try," I smiled. The thing was, Rima was six years old and was to be admitted to grade one, but she had never spoken or heard English at home before. We had to start from scratch. Father assured us that he would be most cooperative and do whatever we told him in his daughter's best interest.

And so, my journey with Rima began.

I should mention here that the rain continued to pour that day, and eventually, it was declared a half-day at school.

Rima joined us at school three days later.

We began with alphabet recognition, sounds, and associations. She was a quick visual learner. Weekly lesson plans were made. Homework was given regularly. We worked with her private tutor, who encouraged her parents to be around when she was taught so they could also pick up important basic words. Homework was schoolwork to be followed up on daily for an hour, with a break in between. We used lots of picture books, magazines, and newspapers to spot the letters through sounds. Phonics, blends, and sight words followed. We made good progress. The Motivational Chart system worked wonders, as we used stars and smileys as incentives. Numbers were learned fast, too. Number concepts through objects and role play were achievable at an age-appropriate level. We faced difficulty in writing. Verbally, she made age-appropriate progress, but we lagged in writing. For grades one and two, she was assessed on her verbal skills, and her written work in the English language was assessed at her level. The worksheets were read to her, and she would attempt to respond. Comprehension skills were fairly on par with the class level, provided the passage or questions were read to her.

She was fond of wafers and potato chips. For the entire first year that Rima joined the school, I remember eating one chip daily from her breakfast box, as she would insist that I get the first chip from her box. She made friends easily, as they all loved chips.

As years went by, her written work got better. Her struggle with spelling continued. In the previous chapters, I covered the tips for working with spellings. Her father conversed in English with us when he visited us, mostly on Open Days after she reached her secondary school section. He mentioned that he would always be ever so grateful for permitting Rima and encouraging him to try to speak English.

She passed her SSC board exams with good results. She completed her HSC board exams. She earned her bachelor's degree in special education and pursued her postgraduate studies.

She chose to work with children with special needs. She says she took this path not only to support students with learning differences but to show them they are capable and valued.

"The whole purpose of education is to turn mirrors into windows."

– Sydney J. Harris

How Attention Deficit Hyperactivity Disorder and Learning Disabilities Played an Important Role

This is an interesting story of Dharini. Dharini never missed school. She paid attention to everything around her, including when she was in the classroom, too. Interestingly, she was smart and was promptly able to respond orally to the questions asked. Her teachers were still very concerned as she disturbed everyone around her. She was unable to sit in her seat for the entire period. She would wiggle in her seat. Nudging her partner was not uncommon. It was easy to spot her under her desk. Her pencils kept falling faster than the leaves of autumn.

Depending on the work being done in the classroom, the subject taught, and her interest level in the subject, teachers had learned to be patient and keep her occupied over time. She was responsible for arranging books in the cupboard, distributing worksheets, and even helping the teachers carry their books.

She was not interested in sports and physical games. Now, this was very challenging as one had to find a means to channel her energy. Her art teacher always praised her, and she would not believe the other teachers when they said she was very hyper. Aha! She was creative, and we found her interest in quilling, and making greeting cards, and charts.

When it came to written work, she always needed to use the washroom. Initially, she was encouraged to complete half of the written work compared to others, and then gradually she learned to complete her task. To avoid completing her written work, she had resorted to lying at home. Her parents were concerned. We had a few sessions together with Dharini and her mother. We worked out study plans with time slots to be followed at home. After every 15 minutes of written work, she was allowed to do a creative activity like quilling or drawing. She had agreed to this. But after a few days, her mother complained again. We realised there was more to her disinterest in writing. She had difficulties with her written work. When corrected, her books looked very red, disturbing her; hence, she preferred not to write. We did some informal assessments and realised she may have specific learning disabilities. She had difficulty with her spelling as well as with written expression. We noticed she had difficulties with mathematics, too, as she avoided problem-solving.

A formal assessment revealed her disabilities and a remedial programme was planned. A programme was planned to be followed at home, too. Her mother was eager to learn and followed up regularly. Dharini was given provisions per the board rules, where she did her lower-level mathematics, and all the provisions were provided in the 9th and 10th grades. She did well and got her provisions in the 12th grade, too. Dharini pursued her passion for creative arts, took up courses in design, and is now working with a famous designer. She continues making paper quilling jewellery and experiments with quilling work, using it to make watches, wall clocks, nameplates, and much more.

Chapter Sixteen

How Our Environment Affects Our Lives

Dilbur was a frail, friendly child studying in grade four. If you can visualise a scene from a Hindi movie, a child from a financially backward home. She looks starved and anaemic. Her mother doesn't speak English but understands it. She does not understand why she doesn't score well in her exams despite her mother trying to teach her. On the open day, her mother Daisy was very upset that she had taught her all the answers asked in the question paper, but still Dilbur failed the test. We looked into the details: study time, study pattern, teaching techniques, any further assistance from outside, and so on. Her answer papers revealed spelling errors and grammatical errors, and jumbled words in the sentences. Missing words and the use of articles unnecessarily were observed in her sentences.

We discussed this in detail and made a programme for her. We also included her father's input, and he was assigned tasks to help Dilbur in her daily study time. Through our sessions, we learned that Dilbur had a younger sibling who was diagnosed with spasticity.

Spasticity is a condition that causes muscles to feel stiff or rigid. It could be a symptom of brain, spinal cord, or motor nerve damage. It could affect speech and movement. It could make it difficult to perform daily activities, depending on the affected body parts and severity.

Kareena, her younger sister, soon got admission to the same school. Kareena adapted well to the school system. She made friends, and fortunately for her, her classmates were very patient with her and readily helped her whenever she needed it.

Dilbur's nature and behaviour were changing. She was concerned about her sister and felt ashamed of her sister's certain behaviours at school. She refused to accept Kareena as her sister because she thought her friends would call her names. Her academic work, which was getting on par with the class level, was again showing a downward curve. She was counselled. Her peers were also involved. We worked regularly, and the two sisters soon became best pals.

As years went by, Dilbur was assessed for specific learning disabilities as she had shown signs earlier, and the remedial programme was already in place. Certification was sorted, and provisions were granted. Dilbur cleared her tenth grade with good results, which her parents were very proud of. She took a great interest in academics and pursued her Bachelor of Arts Degree. She would tutor kids up to grade four to support her family financially. Her interest in supporting kids and affinity towards teaching led her to complete her course in early childhood education (ECCED). She enjoys her work and looks forward to every new day. She says that she learns something new every day. Every kid is amazing. They bring joy to her life.

Kareena was unable to cope with the regular school system. Her parents decided to shift her to a school with special support. Kareena also cleared her grade ten through the Open School system curriculum. Kareena took a great interest in yoga and she is a very regular yoga practitioner. She encouraged many of her friends in her school to practice yoga. She takes pride in showing off her certain yoga asanas to family and friends whenever she gets an opportunity.

To understand the kind of therapy used to help Dilbur cope with her difficulties, the following techniques were used:

Narrative therapy helped her identify strengths and abilities to improve her social anxiety and problem behaviours. We used a goal-oriented approach that helped her discover new skills and knowledge to respond to challenges.

We used narrative therapy to:

- Help her identify strengths and abilities that she was unaware of.
- Help her improve her self-confidence, which helped her deal with the underlying problems.
- Reduce social anxiety.
- Reduce problem behaviours.
- Improve academic performance.

The parents were involved in the therapeutic sessions. Goal-setting and playtime with her sister were planned and organized. Achievable responsibilities were entrusted to her sister, while she, in turn, was guided to respect her own limits and not push herself beyond the boundaries set by Dilbur.

We also used the techniques and approach explained in the earlier chapters for her specific learning difficulties.

"A bend in the road is not the end of the road. Unless you fail to make the turn."

– Helen Keller

Chapter Seventeen

When Self-Doubt Arises

A doctor is God to some, and the same doctor becomes the devil to others. Similarly, there are instances when we hear stories of misdiagnosis or incorrect treatments.

Sunita and Honey were two of my students, my most challenging students, whom I would always keep in mind whenever I see new referrals. They were very smart in everything they did, except in their academic work. They were smart to bully others and very smart not to get bullied by others. Both of them were, unfortunately, misdiagnosed initially. They were sent for assessment. I had suspected that Sunita had specific learning disabilities; she was diagnosed as having only a language barrier. I thought Honey had only difficulties as far as exposure to the English language was concerned, but she was diagnosed as having low-functioning intelligence.

So, programme planning was based on diagnosis, but through experience and the pattern of learning, we did not ignore our beliefs. We considered their strengths and abilities and planned a programme to improve their weaker skills.

After three years, we sent them for reassessment and voilà! The diagnosis said specific learning disabilities for Sunita. Honey's parents were reluctant. They did not go for a reassessment. Honey's parents had to shift residences, and hence, they moved to the suburbs, and Honey left school in the eighth grade. Her mother would consult me occasionally. Honey later finished her tenth and twelfth-grade board exams through the Open School System. Honey took up a certificate course in beautification.

Sunita was very fortunate in terms of her grade ten examinations. The Covid-19 pandemic had hit by then. She was struggling to attend school through online video calls, although individual coaching and assistance were provided. She was finding it extremely difficult to focus online. A lack of supervision and an unfavourable internet connection exacerbated her difficulties. This also led to her accessing multiple online games, which distracted her for hours. We had online meetings with Sunita and her mother. A timetable was planned for her at a time that was convenient and suitable for her. We checked in with Sunita regularly and counselled her as frequently as required. She managed to clear her tenth board exams.

A few chapters ago, I shared what a pleasure it is to know how stories progress and end, even when we aren't longer part of them. This one, however, ends on a cliffhanger. It would have felt nice to be thanked for my efforts, but of course, my students and clients do not owe me anything. But the human being within us would love to be seen and acknowledged. I am glad I could guide, support, and be a part of her school journey. I wish her well always and pray she is safe and doing well for herself in life.

CHAPTER EIGHTEEN

Learning with Comorbidities

"Sejal, stand up! Sejal, Sejal!" Once I was passing by a classroom and I heard the teacher screaming quite loudly. I thought it must be a student not paying attention. A few days later, I heard another teacher saying, "Sejal!" It became imperative to intervene. During recess, I first met Sejal's class teacher and checked if she had noticed anything about Sejal. I remember the teacher's dramatic response vividly: "Oh, Sejal, she never listens to you. She never answers any questions. She even goes to sleep after the first recess itself." I then met the teachers who were seeking her attention in the classroom. They said she was acting strangely and never responded when her name was called immediately. They too mentioned that it seems she is not interested in studies. "She is too arrogant," another teacher remarked.

I had never met Sejal, but I felt that something was amiss. I sent a note to her class teacher to send Sejal to visit me for the first time. She was neatly dressed. Her hair was neatly tied in a high ponytail. She sought permission to enter my room. She sat right in front of me. I asked her about likes and dislikes. I asked if she knew why I wished to see her. She said she was not sure, and maybe some teacher complained that she left her notes incomplete. You would be surprised to see her reaction when I told her the true reason. "I heard your teachers call your name loudly on many occasions when I passed by your classroom." Her mouth was wide open for a very long time in disbelief. She joked and said, "Ma'am, I really didn't know that they shout so loudly." We spoke for a while, and she left. As she left, I called her name, and she never looked back. It was at that moment that I confirmed my doubt that she genuinely couldn't hear. We called her parents, spoke to them, and requested that they get her hearing checked. The test results revealed that she suffered from hearing loss in one ear. She was fitted for a hearing aid. Her hearing got better, boredom disappeared, and academic work improved—Just like that!

Reflections for the reader:

Dear readers, if you know of someone who has a hearing impairment, how would you support this person?

CHAPTER NINETEEN

Nina and Her OCD

Nina was referred to me by a dear friend. I saw her at my clinic. She was eight. Her eyes were full of mischief. These small buttons of brown eyes moved in all directions. My friend mentioned that Nina is a curious child; she is very inquisitive, she can't sit in one place, and she hates to write.

Nina walked in with her mother and reached out straight to a stuffed pup seated on my side table. After a bit, she requested that I show her the washroom. Her mother and I continued our talk. She came out and greeted me with a smile. We discussed her favourite subjects, interests, and things she did not like. Of course, she mentioned she did not like to write. She asked me why it is important to write. "Mummy always says it is important to write and write fast. But I don't like to write. Why should I write?" She twinkled her eyes and looked at me expecting a favourable response. I continued, showing her some coloured ruled pages and pointing at her a box of pens, pencils, and erasers. I said, "Sweetheart, I understand you do not like to write, would you please make a list of things you don't like?" She took her time to select a coloured pencil. She chose a dark blue pencil. She began her task, thinking and pausing, and wrote very neatly. She made a mistake, and she was stuck. She used an eraser, and the page turned blue and messy. We could see that she was feeling upset. Now she used her finger to clean it. "Aaah! I want to wash my hands." She ran to the washroom. She returned, staring at her fingers and rubbing them. I noticed she was uncomfortable. This time she decided to write with a regular pencil. She requested to go to the washroom again. I asked her mother if she had noticed similar behaviour at home. Her mother poured her heart out. She said it was a big concern especially when she is outdoors or when they visit friends or family.

I met Nina for almost six months regularly, once a week. It was fun to work with Nina. We used different techniques. We realised the reasons behind avoiding writing. We also noticed that she wanted her work to be perfect. Our Nina was very creative and very cooperative. Once she understood the nuances, she was more receptive, and we were a great team to work together.

How therapy worked:

A weekly programme was planned.

We used a lot of fun games with words and letters.

We began by only writing single words, saying five words a day for the first week.

Then moved on to five sentences and so on.

To avoid making her work messy by erasing, she was given clues to help her form sentences, or help was provided for difficult spellings.

Parental support was essential to help her deal with her difficulties.

In our narratives, we used her favourite characters, Elsa and Ariel, to work through our repetitive thoughts and compulsive behaviours.

Like Elsa, she would create magical powers to make her writing beautiful and interesting.

She says she will be courageous like Ariel and make sure she does her best.

Nina still struggles with her hand-cleaning routine, but I can proudly say that her determination and resilience have helped her understand the difficulties she faces. She has learned to delay the urge or the need to clean her hands often. She has adapted to a few techniques that she feels no longer cause her anxiety, and her parents feel that they no longer feel embarrassed when they visit family or friends.

CHAPTER TWENTY

How I Learned to Live with OCD

Kanishka's mother sent me a text message saying that she sensed her daughter needed help, as she felt that she was "behaving a bit weird." She booked an appointment, and we met at our clinic. Kanishka was accompanied by her mother, Durga. Kanishka appeared friendly, but I felt she was uncomfortable about something. My thoughts were whether she was forced to visit me, or if her mother was making up stories. We soon started talking. Kanishka is in her 30s, lives with her parents, is educated, has a good job, and loves to travel. She has been to many places and is a solo traveller. So why was she visiting me? I said, "I envy you, but I want to know what is troubling you. You seem to be disturbed about something. Do you wish to speak with me privately?"

"The thing is, I am very concerned about certain behaviours I have adopted. I know it is strange, but I can't help myself getting attracted towards these behaviours, and my thoughts keep racing towards that act, or my body freezes at times," she informed me in one breath. Aha! It seems a cat passed across her path just before she entered our clinic premises. (It is a myth or a belief by some that when a cat crosses your path in front of you, it brings bad luck.) She had to take a turn around, and fortunately, she spotted another point of entry and made it to the session, of course, a few minutes late.

Now, this explains the discomfort. We spoke about the things that caused her worry. She was very verbal and concerned about the direction in which her life was going because of all these worries. She was certain she didn't need all of this in her life. She mentioned her compulsiveness and was wondering if she had OCD.

Obsessive-Compulsive Disorder, or OCD, as it is known, can be explained as a mental health condition that causes people to experience recurring intrusive thoughts and repetitive behaviours. Obsessions are intrusive, uncontrollable, and irrational thoughts or images that can cause anxiety. Compulsions are repetitive behaviours that people perform to relieve the distress caused by intrusive thoughts.

Durga had her thoughts and shared her opinions. She mentioned how gradually, over the past few months, Kanishka had become troubled by her obsessions and how the entire family was being affected.

Using narrative therapy, we tried to create a more flexible vision of herself and the future. Our goal was to help her develop a more cohesive identity and break away from being defined by her troubles. We created new mental images and meanings by addressing the unique narratives that were built. We worked on developing internal strength and responsiveness by externalising dominant problems. Therapy was combined with breathing techniques, visualisation, and mindfulness. Practising affirmations and gratefulness was encouraged.

Of course, the final goal is to be free from "these repeated behaviours" but we saw great progress in delaying the urge to engage in compulsive behaviours or paying attention to obsessions. Many stories unfolded, and we worked on them and built narratives. She was most receptive to the therapy. There were some doubts about therapy, there were myths attached to behaviours, and there were dominant stories causing distress. The preferred stories were explored. These stories reflected the values she believed in, her strengths, and the hopes she had for life. They helped to navigate her life in a positive direction.

Chapter Twenty-One

Procrastination

Rishi came along with his mother to me. He was tall and lean. His eyes appeared worried, as though he were seeking answers to many questions.

His mother gave a little background for their visit. Rishi was 17. We spoke about his concerns, hopes, and dreams. It was essential to let Rishi know that he was not the problem, but the problem was the problem. He seemed confused, but as the session progressed, he was able to open up. He let me know that it had been ages since he had spoken to someone for so long. He was amazed to notice a change in himself.

We fixed a timeslot for another session. He entered with a cute, adorable smile. I asked him the secret behind this smile. He said he kept his appointment and did not postpone it. That was a strange response that definitely needed exploration.

We learned about his habit of delaying or pushing things to be done later. There were many stories, and therapy went on for a while. One story was about procrastination.

Honestly, I am a victim of procrastination myself. This book would have been ready a few years ago had I not procrastinated. Well, many of us are aware that procrastination is known as putting things off to be done later, pushing them away to be done tomorrow, until we realise the "tomorrow" doesn't come at all. We all procrastinate from time to time.

For Rishi, as I mentioned, as the stories unfolded, we learned about his fears, his inability to reach out to friends, and the thoughts that told him, "What if?"

"What if he thinks I am stupid?" "What if they think I am talking nonsense?" "What if they start judging me?"

Rishi was made aware of the reason behind procrastination. He noticed he needed external validation to know his worth. There was self-doubt, and he would question his performance. Tackling important tasks induced fears. We worked on his fears—fears of inadequate performance and potential. As therapy continued, it was essential to help him plan, practice, and monitor the desired outcome. Goals were set. An action plan was developed with the resources required to reach the goals. Regularly reviewing the progress and celebrating achievements was essential. It was not a smooth sail. Barriers of doubt were identified and addressed with feedback, guidance, and encouragement to reach the desired outcomes.

Certain questions that helped enrich and evaluate his preferred stories were:

What does this story tell you about yourself?

How does this story make you feel?

When you are living according to this story, would you say something about its benefits?

If people around you had to say what Rishi is like now, what would they say?

How can you make this story influential and visible in your life? Is there an image that you could describe?

Reflections for the reader:

You may have put off certain things to be done later. What is your story? Can you think about a time when you procrastinated? How would you change that?

Ask yourself some of the questions you read above and see what stories come up for you.

Chapter Twenty-Two

Sympathy Versus Empathy

"Do you know Mary, this new girl in our school, poor thing, she doesn't have a mother. She is so weak in academic work, but still, I gave her admission."

"Poor fellow, Sunita's father, he works so hard but pays no attention to her."

"Oh dear! Don't disturb her, she is not interested. We will see about it later."

"Here, take this money, I'll pay for her tuition too, but she will not manage with her academics, let's get her admitted to another school."

When you hear such words, you are certain there is so much pity. But what are the thoughts of the person who is part of the conversation? Are they going to be comfortable? Do they even need your pity?

I believe people do not need pity or even sympathy. One should be EMPATHETIC rather than sympathetic.

Things one could do to be empathetic:

Be a good listener. Do not be judgmental. Let them express their feelings and perspectives.

Others may feel a certain way or have disagreements, so encourage them to express their perspective. Paraphrase your questions and help others voice their concerns. Empathy helps build stronger connections and improve efficient learning.

The tone of voice, our body language, and facial expressions can also express empathy. Smiling often makes you feel good and makes others more comfortable. It builds trust and strengthens relationships.

Once you learn to be empathetic, you and everyone around you will lead a satisfying life. In a world where people are used to picking flaws, finding faults, and creating anger, this skill of empathy will help soothe the situation.

Another important thing to remember is not to be judgmental. Before passing judgment, think of the situation the person is in, ask yourself a few questions, and find out some of the unique stories that person could share with you by framing your questions well. Keep in mind the importance of body posture, facial expressions, a gentle, comforting tone, and appropriate use of touch.

"When you start to develop your powers of empathy and imagination, the whole world opens up to you."

– Susan Sarandon

Reflections for the reader:

As simple as all this sounds, it takes us years to learn and practice, yet we still falter at these skills even as therapists. Not everyone needs to train to be a therapist, empathetic, and non-judgmental. I remember my daughter sharing something her trainer spoke about on a course. Dr. Windy Dryden, an exceptional Rational Emotive Behaviour Therapy and Single Session Therapy practitioner and trainer talked about how everyday interaction or an experience could also be "therapeutic", although it occurs outside of "therapy". Spend some time thinking about what this could mean. What experiences have you had that were therapeutic for you? How could you use empathy and a non-judgmental approach to provide that for someone else?

CHAPTER TWENTY-THREE

Technology at its Best

One of the darkest phases of everyone's life is the COVID phase.

Initially, we heard of COVID-19 at school, and most of us were thrilled to know that schools were shut. Of course, we enjoyed our time at home with family by our side, each doing their bit to keep each other entertained. Then started the cooking phase. Experiments began, and postings on social media of who did what, who cooked what, and who ate what began. This happiness was very short-lived. Once we realised the gravity of the situation and how every individual was coping, we soon learned how severe the virus was and its effects; none of us knew what would happen. Our concern was our school's students, their families, and how everyone coped. Many parents were in a special task force, either doctors or some medical professionals, who had to report for duty. Soon, technology came to our rescue. We learned Zoom and Google Meet. We learned to make PowerPoint presentations. I am very grateful to our patient teachers who taught us the use of technology in detail. We learned of our shortcomings and our hidden talents.

Our students came to our homes, and we went to theirs. It was a wonderful virtual world. Some students were privileged with their private rooms without outside disturbances, while a few barely managed to share a table.

The feelings were mixed. There was excitement; there was sadness. It was easier to reach out to students, but few needed constant attention and support. We learned to be even more patient than before. It was interesting to note how our very own students would guide us using appropriate tech-savvy tools when we were at the learning stage.

The transition from offline (in-person) to online had its challenges, but the education system focused on digital learning. Technology increased learner engagement, although a few learners took maximum advantage of this technology negatively.

> **"Technology is just a tool. In terms of getting the kids working together and motivating them, the teacher is the most important."**
>
> **– Bill Gates**

> **"Technology will never replace great teachers, but technology in the hands of great teachers is transformational."**
>
> **– George Couros**

Reflections for the reader:

Do you belong to a generation that knew what the world was before televisions, landline telephones, or cellular phones existed? Or do you belong to a generation that literally saw the world change with technology? Or were you born with a phone in your hand, as they say?

Sure, we can debate the boon and bane of technological advancement. However, in my experience working across age groups, I realise that better-adjusted adults and older adults are the ones who remain curious and willing to adapt to changing technologies. Reflect on your hesitations to try something new that may not have existed when you were younger.

CHAPTER TWENTY-FOUR

The Gifted

Some years ago, one pleasant evening, I met Soham with his parents. Both his parents had jobs that kept them busy. They were highly educated and had responsible positions at their jobs.

Soham's mother mentioned that he was a very introverted child and interacted with very few people. He was not interested in meeting or making friends with his age group. His father added that recently, he started showing defiant behaviour and became rude to them. They were not sure how to reach out to him, as they were getting complaints from school, too. He had an argument with his school teacher, for which he was reprimanded too. Apparently, the math teacher was explaining a new concept, and before the teacher could finish his explanation, Soham blurted out the answer. This happened thrice, which made the teacher furious and led to a heated argument.

We had a lengthy conversation. Since the age of four, his parents had noticed that he was a very quick learner. His parents had put him in various classes like chess and dramatics. He would blurt out dialogues by himself, but would not enjoy performing. He read books. Comics never interested him. He was curious and asked many questions. He had stopped attending dramatics classes but continued with chess. He would compete with older kids. At times when he would lose against someone, he would throw tantrums. They said, "He was a bad loser." Their concern was his behaviour, and they needed guidance to be able to support his needs.

As suggested by their paediatrician, an intelligence assessment was done. His Intelligence Quotient was quoted to be in the moderately gifted range.

IQ or Intelligence Quotient was originally measured by taking the ratio of a person's mental age to chronological age and multiplying it by 100. This means that it measures relative intelligence. It compares your performance on a test to others of your age. Certain standardised tests are designed to assess human intelligence, abilities, and potential. These numbers are further broken into categories like: 69 and below, which are categorised as extremely low intelligence. Between 70 and 79 is the borderline category, 80 and 89 is low average, 90 and 114 is average intelligence, and 115 and 129 is above average. 130 to 144 is moderately gifted, and 145 to 159 is highly gifted.

It is important to note that an IQ number may tell a story, but not always the entire story. At times, it may be useful to know, but not always. To explain this statement, some essential factors like the ability to learn from situations, manage difficult situations, or be involved as an important team member are not considered. People with a higher IQ are often unable to meet social norm expectations, or they even find it difficult to converse with people around them. Similarly, people with a lower IQ score may be able to function better in social situations. You may have heard of EQ or EI, which is Emotional Intelligence. As the name suggests, EI is the ability to understand or manage emotions.

There is Social Intelligence (SQ) too, which is being aware of social interactions. It could be explained as the ability of a person to understand and manage relationships with others. We also know of AQ or an Adversity Quotient, which measures a person's ability to deal with adversities in life (Understanding the different types of intelligence: IQ, EQ, SQ and AQ, 2025).

Reflections for readers:

Do you know of other theories that propose different kinds of intelligence? Can you think of what they might be? Look them up if you are really curious to know more.

My knowledge about 'giftedness' was limited at that time. He fit into the superior intelligence category. I knew that the gifted have a good sense of memory; they could easily retain and recall information. That explained the memory and blurting out dialogues for Soham. I also knew they got bored easily, which could have been a major trigger that may have led to an argument with the teacher.

With my limited knowledge and experience, I did not wish to experiment with Soham. I did suggest a few techniques and ways to make their conversations and interactions interesting and meaningful. The idea of giving space and time to Soham to understand his needs was welcomed by them.

It was important for the parents to recognise his abilities and understand his intellectual and emotional needs. They were advised to seek assistance from a professional educationist or psychologist specialising in giftedness.

After Soham, I did a lot of reading and research on managing 'the gifted'.

Things that one should know:

These students are quite sensitive, and this may lead to frustration easily. They may lean towards perfectionism, which may make them anxious. They may not necessarily excel in all areas of development, which would lead to differences in cognitive, physical, and emotional development.

One should aim to provide the right support, guidance, and resources by creating a stimulating environment.

Whether a child is gifted or not, when parents engage with their children, support their educational needs, adapt to their learning environment, and share their power of resilience, there is immense joy and satisfaction. This would help the child reach his/her potential, reflecting the success of their nurturing efforts.

Reflection for the reader:

Do you think our education system is equipped to manage all types of students in a classroom situation? What changes would you suggest to make our classrooms inclusive?

Have you heard of anyone who has a superior or very high IQ? How would a day in the life of a 'gifted' person look to you?

What are your thoughts on having an IQ assessment?

Chapter Twenty-Five

Importance of Therapy

"Catch them young." "Never delay the process." "When in doubt, seek help."

In the earlier chapters, we read about stigmatisation, gratefulness, and acceptance.

It is strange to hear from parents when they speak about their own kids, how the child struggles while writing, or how the child is unable to sustain attention. They mention that their child keeps banging his head, but they fail to recognise the need to check or find out why such behaviour occurs. The understanding is always that, "Oh, he is just a kid; he will outgrow the behaviour."

I have worked with all age groups, be they males or females. Every person has their own identity and uniqueness. Every individual learns and understands differently. Yes, there will be a therapeutic process and a plan with short-term and long-term goals. However, therapy will differ according to individual needs.

My approach is very versatile. I use an integrated multi-sensory approach. Therapy sessions are fun and holistic, too. When connecting with parents, students, or individuals, we take a detailed history including likes, dislikes, daily schedule, food habits, sensitivity to texture, sleep patterns, and the amount of quality time spent together. Vitamins play an important role, so questions about vitamin or mineral deficiencies are also asked.

I value breathing exercises, brain gym, and Audiblox. I also incorporate visualisation/mindfulness practices. My yoga practices have deepened my awareness and created space for mental calmness. I incorporate my yoga learnings into therapy as well. I encourage saying affirmations regularly and ending one's day by being grateful.

For my dear readers, I request that you practice saying at least three affirmations every morning. It could be as simple as:

I am strong.

I am brave.

I believe in myself.

I am capable.

I love and accept myself.

Practice gratitude by maintaining a gratitude journal or a gratitude jar. Every night, before you go to bed, you must think of at least three things that you are grateful for on that particular day. It could be any simple thing, but one must make a good attempt to think of their entire day and either write it down or say it orally.

I am grateful to my friend who helped me with my homework.

I am grateful to my friend who listened to me patiently.

I am grateful to the cab driver who drove safely, and I reached home in time to watch my favourite show on television.

I am grateful to my maid who made a delicious soup for me.

I am grateful to my students because of whom I could write this book.

Chapter Twenty-Six

Making Our Classrooms Inclusive – Living in an Inclusive Society

Imagine you are in a park, enjoying the cool breeze. The sun is shining on the leaves of a pipal tree (Bodhi tree). The branches of the pipal tree are growing on the Ashoka tree. You look up at the tree and see the parrots, mynas, crows, bulbuls, coppersmiths, and a squirrel family living together on the same tree. Not to forget hundreds of tiny crawlies on it. Aren't you blessed to witness this? Nature at its best! All-inclusive. Providing shelter for all.

Suddenly, you hear a kid cry. Other kids rush to help him stand on his feet. Mr. Venkat, who was enjoying the cool breeze, was curious to know what had happened. Ram, his friend who was in his wheelchair, explains the scene in detail to him. Wow! We are certainly moving towards being inclusive.

Inclusion: My understanding of inclusion is that people are respected and given the same opportunities irrespective of their backgrounds. Inclusion also means providing accommodations to enable access to the same opportunities.

Similarly, an inclusive society would be a society that includes all its members irrespective of their age, gender, abilities, religion, and sexual orientation. It would be a society that not only provides a culture of inclusivity through communication but also has accessible infrastructure, assistive technology, and support services.

To explain this thought, consider an advertisement,

Vacancy

The following positions are open to all.

Junior accountancy assistant.

Senior position in marketing.

Personal secretary.

Candidates should have knowledge of the work.

Be present for the interview on [Date] at [Time]

Rehan was all excited; he was ready with his resume and all dressed up for his interview. He reached the venue before the scheduled time. However, he could not access the room at the office site as there was no provision for his wheelchair to enter the building.

Would we call this being inclusive?

Moving on to a classroom situation, we have learned about Lyla, Fiona, and Anil, among many more.

Imagine a classroom where all of them are together, along with forty more students. The teacher enters the classroom. Raj is having some trouble letting go of Rahul's collar. Tina is excited to show off the new pencil box her aunt got for her. There is way too much noise. Despite the commotion, Rohan is staring out the window without blinking.

Scene 1:

Nina, the teacher, is furious. She enters the classroom shouting at the students. "Is this a fish market? What is wrong with this class? Are you listening to me?" She bangs her table, adding to the noise. But she manages to get their attention, and all are quiet. They look at her with no interest and continue with the chatter again.

Scene 2:

Nehal, the teacher, takes a deep breath. She goes to the green board and writes, "Good morning, my dear students." She says in a calm voice, "I see that each of you has something to share. I can feel your excitement, and I am curious to know all about it. Before we begin, may we all stand up, stretch our hands high up, and go up, up, up on our toes." All start giggling. "Now let's grow small, let's become as tiny as we can be. Tiny, tiny, tiny." All begin to bend and squat. "Now, stand up! Good morning, everyone."

"Good morning, ma'am," they all wished together with a smile. Nehal continues to be assertive. Place your notebooks on your desk. I need just a pencil and an eraser with you. I will give you exactly five minutes to express yourselves in any form, either writing, sketching, or doodling your feelings or thoughts on the book. Go on. Once you are done, put your notebooks on my table and sit up straight." She then continues with her lesson. She comes prepared to class with her lesson plan. She is aware of her students' abilities. She gets worksheets for all. She has made different worksheets for Lyla and Fiona at their functional level.

Nehal created a welcoming environment where the students felt valued, regardless of their needs or abilities. She provided the necessary support, created a positive environment, and ensured that students participated actively in the classroom.

Was it a difficult task?

As we value the teacher's role in making our classrooms inclusive, we should take up the responsibility to enrich our society and make it inclusive.

A teacher who encourages an inclusive environment would be a good listener, be able to communicate well, adapt to situations, collaborate with students, other teachers, or professionals involved, be empathetic, and manage to keep their students actively engaged. The students would feel valued and respected and have a positive self-image.

Similarly, as a part of an inclusive society, we can contribute in various ways. Educating people and creating awareness should be the most important part of an inclusion programme. How various birds lived together on the two trees growing together, similarly, if only we humans were tolerant of our diverse cultures and needs, understood individual abilities, and learned to value and respect individuals regardless of their differences, this world would be an all-inclusive place to thrive.

"Learn to enjoy and respect each other's differences."

– Fred Meijer

"In diversity, there is beauty and there is strength."

– Maya Angelou

Chapter Twenty-seven

Reflections

"Life isn't about finding yourself. Life is about creating yourself."

– George Bernard Shaw

"What you do makes a difference, and you have to decide what kind of difference you want to make."

– Jane Goodall

I consider myself to be well-grounded and down-to-earth. But when you hear from your very old students or clients on your birthday or Teacher's Day, I am definitely on a high. That feeling is unexplainable. The joy you get when you hear them and talk to them is immense. There is always a tear of joy and pride too. This is the greatest gift! I consider myself blessed to have been associated with such wonderful people.

After my internship, as a fresher, at my new job as a special needs teacher, I was a junior assistant special educator. The senior teacher would guide me and encourage me to make worksheets for the students. There were very few students with whom I worked initially, and it turned out to be fun. My colleagues were supportive too. When it came to meeting up with parents, I would address them as aunty or uncle. My good friend pointed out that some of these 'aunties' may be younger than me or maybe my age. "If you have to, say Mr. so and so or Mrs. so and so," she suggested.

Soon, I took up a job closer to home where, at times, I would continue to address someone as 'aunty/uncle' until I realised I had become a mother myself! It was time for me to check with the person if I could address them by their first name or how they would like me to address them. Something I finally learned. :) Decades later, I had to teach my own daughter the same thing. Now that's something that makes you feel old!

This was not the only thing I learned. Over three decades, I have learned to be tolerant, gentle, and patient. I learned to set boundaries and respect every individual, whether the person is senior to you or a tiny toddler. To be honest, I understood so many concepts and topics only after I started teaching. To be able to teach the students the way they learn or understand, we have to experience them first. That is, we have to fit ourselves into their shoes.

I became creative, creating ideas and experimenting with different approaches to my teaching style. I not only learned about current trends and technology from them, but I also learned to be an active listener. The power of resilience. By encouraging them and, many times, challenging them and guiding them to believe in themselves, as well as making them aware of their abilities. Despite the challenges and failures, just by reinforcing them, it was amazing to see how persistent they would be. How would they adapt to learning new techniques, overcome challenges, and bounce back?

I am truly honoured to have had the opportunity to pen this book.

Buddha said, "What we think, we become,"

and

Mahatma Gandhi said, "Be the change you wish to see in the world."

Hear it from the Students

I salute my students for their courage, hope, strength, and determination. Let's hear their stories of resilience in their own words.

(1)

"Firstly, let's start with making the word 'dyslexia' a very normal thing in today's world. It's not something that a child should be labelled as backward or handicapped. So when I was in standard one or two, my class teacher, on a fine day, called my mother to school. She happened to say that her daughter, who is me, is a slow learner in school. At that time (20 years back), this word, dyslexia or slow learner, was SHOCKING. It was surprising for my mother to hear that about her child. So, when my mother heard that I was a slow learner, by God's grace, she never panicked or gave up on me as a child, and that's when a miracle came into our lives. Mrs. Kashmira Kakalia. I can't express how deeply I am grateful to her, as she is one of the kindest teachers who has put in so much effort and helped me overcome my difficulties in studies. I remember that Marathi as a subject was so difficult for me that she guided me to take up a vocational subject instead. After all the hard work and push by her, today I am working for an investment bank in a Manager Position, and I give credit to her for my success.

Ever grateful,
– Fariba"

(2)

"When we speak about learning disabilities in particular, the subject is quite subjective, but also a common case. At least out of 10, you will find five with learning disabilities. This is subjective because it depends on how the individual is able to face daily challenges when thrown at them. There are common victims of bullying. Personally, it was beneficial, but it was also something I would get bullied or teased at for being slow or not attentive, with words like 'Hey, you LD are not invited'. 'You are an LD, so you are so dumb'. 'So dumb'; these phrases are heard constantly by those who are not in the 'norm', but I would say being a learning-disabled child was also a good advantage. I had the advantage of being able to opt for subjects that felt comfortable and learning something new. I don't think I could have done algebra in school; it's way above my level, haha! However, with age, I slowly stopped relying on the LD factors and purely started to live on instincts and train my brain. In college, I only opted for a writer for Sanskrit as it was a mandatory subject in my college, and Sanskrit was difficult to cope with, so to make it easy, I used my LD provisions and passed my board exams in 12th grade. It is both an advantage and a horror to me, but with age, as I grew up, I saw that not all were bullies, and it was okay to be called an LD student. I also started to come to terms with who I was and who I am. Looking back, all the sad feelings I had in school for being bullied are just vague memories and nothing more as I learn to embrace them.

Confident,
– Nayhid"

(3)

"At a very early age, I was diagnosed with a learning disability, which included dyslexia, Dyscalculia, and Dysgraphia. I couldn't understand what I read, I couldn't calculate the way others used to, I used to stammer while answering, and I was too slow in writing. Bullying was very common. I was asked to read out loud by other classmates, and whenever I stumbled on a word, all the other students would laugh out loud."

I was introduced to Mrs. Kakalia during my senior kindergarten due to my learning disability, and since then, she has stayed and supported me for over 10 years. She has always been patient with me and everyone who is having the same or worse difficulties than mine. Mrs. Kakalia will always hold a special place in my life, as she patiently supported me and paved a path for me to walk on flawlessly.

She taught me strategies to navigate the chaos of letters that refused to align, the frustration of numbers that danced out of place, and the overwhelming jumble of thoughts that never seemed to make it onto the page. Slowly, with her support, I started to see my learning differences not as weaknesses, but as a part of who I was—a part that could be managed, understood and even worked with.

I remember when I was in second grade, I was bullied by some classmates for months, making going to school a nightmare, and I started giving reasons for skipping school. My parents turned to Mrs. Kakalia as I was scared to tell them about the bullying; she stood by me and helped me fight my bullies. Mrs. Kakalia has been and will always be the most special person in my life, and I will always be grateful to her for believing in me and helping me to be stronger and achieve greater things in my life.

– Vividha"

(4)

"We, Zarthostis, accommodate ourselves everywhere, but Kashmira openly invites old senior citizens to join her classes. Initially, we were about 20 in number; later, the group grew. We enjoyed attending her sessions, doing light exercises, playing fun games, improving our memories, and exploring our creative sides. We enjoyed it as we met so many people. We looked forward to attending these sessions. So coolly, she welcomed us with her polite and sweet voice, full of love. I would never want to miss her sessions, but my ill health does not permit me. A big thank you to our dear Kashmira."

Regards,
– Bami"

(5)

"It was in 2018 when I heard that Kashmira Kakalia had started her classes (Mental Health Enrichment Programme) for Seniors to keep their minds and bodies happy and healthy. Initially, approximately 20 of us joined, but as the word spread around, many others joined her class.

Kashmira taught us various physical as well as brain exercises to keep us agile, both in body and mind. We all enjoyed her class and the interaction we had with all our friends.

Kashmira shared her knowledge, time, and skills, which have truly impacted the lives of us seniors. We show our appreciation by practising what she taught us daily. She is an exceptional teacher, and her ability to impart her knowledge is very impressive. Her dedication and passion for teaching are evident in all we know and practice.

A few years later, she started her online classes on the GETSETUP platform, and seniors from all over India joined her class.

I will always recommend her to others who will benefit from her expertise.

May God bless her and her family always...

– Anahita"

(6)

"Dyslexia in 2001 had very low acceptance in India. That year, my family and I found out that I am dyslexic. I was very fortunate as my science tutor was well aware of learning disabilities, as he had worked with students having specific learning disabilities in the school where he worked. I was in the ninth grade when I was diagnosed with specific learning disabilities. My mom was aware of it and had accepted it, but not my father. However, later on, as he read up more and became aware of the causes, symptoms, and therapy, he accepted it. It is said it is never too late, as the diagnosis helped me during my 10th grade. My school teachers and principal supported my parents to help me get the credits the SSC board would give at that time. My life changed after that, and I became more confident. In college, I became a better student and quite an extrovert. I completed my undergraduate as well as my MBA from a good university. Did my hardships and dyslexia go away? No, but it is part of life. I faced issues while at my college and had to work harder than normal students. I settled in the U.S.A. and work as a credit analyst at a bank. I am a good analyst, but I get stuck in the flow, and that is again due to dyslexia, which hampers my performance. People think you have good grades and degrees, so you have overcome dyslexia. But dyslexia is a part of me. I have accepted my dyslexia, and I understand my strengths and shortcomings. I am persistent and do not let dyslexia stand in my way.

– Payal"

(7)

"Growing up, I always felt like I was falling behind. Words on a page never seemed to stay still, and no matter how hard I tried, reading, writing, and numbers felt like a battle I could never win. I remember the frustration of watching my classmates breeze through assignments and lessons while I struggled just to make sense of a sentence or a math problem. It made me doubt myself; was I just not smart enough?

Then, I met Kashmira Miss when I joined another school in the seventh grade. She didn't see me as a kid who struggled; she saw me as someone who could. Instead of getting frustrated, she was patient. She found ways to teach me that made sense—breaking words apart, using colours, and reading aloud together. She taught me that my brain wasn't broken; it just worked differently.

Slowly, as I progressed through grades, things changed. I started reading with more confidence. Writing didn't feel as scary. But more than that, I stopped seeing myself as not good enough. She made me believe that I was capable, that my struggles didn't define me, and that I had something valuable to offer.

Looking back, I realise she didn't just help me with dyslexia; she changed the way I saw myself. Today, it is because of her patience and support that I could work through life, pursuing my MBA and currently being in a middle management position with a reputed bank, and for that, I'm eternally grateful to Kashmira Miss.

– Rhea"

(8)

"As a mother, when I first got to know about my daughter being diagnosed as dyslexic, very honestly, I was quite nervous, confused, and felt very helpless. Whenever she read a sentence, she would find it difficult to complete. Numbers, too, were difficult to understand. In her previous school, most teachers would get upset with her without explaining the issue. She started making excuses for not wanting to go to school or wanting to come back home from school. Exam times were the most challenging and stressful. She switched schools in the seventh grade. Things started looking up and brighter. With Kashmira coaching and guiding her, she recognised her strengths and weaknesses. She started enjoying what she was doing, and I think the encouragement she got was the most important part. It wasn't an easy journey, but a fulfilling one. A special child needs encouragement, patience, and understanding, which I learned much later in her journey. Grateful to Kashmira and all the teachers. Today, my daughter is a confident woman."

(9)

"Before I had my own kids, I worked at a preschool as an honorary teacher. In a fun way and behaving like one of them, I would entertain these kids and keep them occupied. In the meantime, I saw all the kids reciting Jack and Jill rhymes, but my own kindergarten child refused to remember any poems. I was shocked to see them remember everything but studies, including the alphabet. Eventually, someone told me to take them to Wadia Hospital, where they do certain tests for such kids. I did as was told by this friend and came to know of the term dyslexia. At the hospital, they began therapy, which included games to improve concentration. My husband refused to believe what was going on, arguing that our kids were mischievous. I took them to therapy, but in those days, it was still difficult for me to afford them privately. Finally, our school introduced us to the special educator Kashmira Kakalia, who would help my child. It was a tough road, but the provisions assisted them in clearing their examinations.

– Rashna"

(10)

"In the grand year of 1995, I arrived in the world—a tiny, clueless baby, blissfully unaware of the rollercoaster ahead. My parents were overjoyed, basking in the glow of new parenthood, blissfully unaware that life had a plot twist in store. Fast forward a few years, and there I was, a child who never quite found joy in studying. While other kids scribbled down notes enthusiastically, I doodled in the margins, my mind wandering to places far more interesting than math textbooks.

Then came 2005—fifth standard. The year everything changed. A diagnosis. Learning disability. My parents, hearing those words for the first time, were shocked. How? Why? What does this mean? Questions swirled; anxiety loomed. But amidst the uncertainty, one thing became clear—they would do whatever it took to support me. Enter Mrs. Kakalia, our guiding light, our rock. With her support, my parents navigated this uncharted territory, reshaping their lives around and making my academic journey smoother. They spoke to countless people in their quest for answers, desperate for reassurance. And then, oh, the irony—someone told them: "Nothing to worry about! The world is open to her... except she can't be a doctor. Anything else is possible." Well, life had other plans. Because here I am—Dr. Devanshi. Not the kind that prescribes medicine, but definitely the kind that assigns essays and deadlines.

This journey was far from easy. I can still picture my parents' tears—first, tears of fear when they worried whether I would even pass my 10th board exams, and later, tears of overwhelming pride as they watched me graduate with a PhD. It has been nothing short of a rollercoaster for all of us. Even now, my father can't stop crying out of sheer happiness, while my mother dances her heart out, telling the world, "My daughter is a doctor now!" The same daughter whose teachers once called her parents to school to complain—too naughty, too distracted, never paying attention. And yet, here I am. Back in school, stigma kept us silent—we didn't talk about my diagnosis. Today, I stand in front of students as a lecturer in psychology at the University of Greenwich, London, proving that no label or expectation can define what we are truly capable of.

This journey isn't mine alone—it belongs to my parents, who never stopped believing in me. Every time I sign my name, I make sure to include their names with me, as you see below. If you're still reading this, let this be your reminder—If I can do it, you can too! Believe in yourself, because sometimes, that's all it takes to change everything.

– Dr. Devanshi Hansu Niren Vikamsey
BA, MA, MSc, PhD and counting…"

(11)

"The journey of being a student with a learning disability has been one of resilience, self-discovery, and growth. School was not always easy—making friends sometimes felt like a challenge, and there were moments of isolation. Yet, amidst those moments, I also found kindness in those who truly saw me for who I was.

There were times when I felt overwhelmed, wondering where I belonged and what my future would look like. Doubts crept in, and self-esteem wavered as I struggled with academic expectations and the fear of not measuring up. I often questioned whether I would find my place in the world. But as time passed, I began to embrace my insecurities instead of letting them define me. I learned that my worth was not tied to grades or comparisons but to the effort I put in and the progress I made. Navigating academic challenges and societal perceptions was not easy, but those experiences shaped me in many ways. They lit a spark within me—a desire to help others who might be feeling the same way. That realisation led me to pursue a path as a special educator, not only to support students with learning differences but to show them that they are capable, valued, and never alone.

This journey has been sweet and difficult, filled with moments of doubt and triumph. Through it all, I have learned to stand up for myself, recognise my own strengths, and continue pushing forward. Every challenge has taught me something, and if there is one thing I now know for certain, it's that perseverance and self-acceptance can lead to incredible growth.

– Ritika Yadav"

(12)

"This is my story of how I came so far in life, managing serious learning disabilities. Not only did I graduate, but I managed to make many friends. Fortunately, my ability to think clearly and efficiently was not impaired by my handicap, although it made academic achievement a challenge. My perceptual problems include visual, auditory, and motor modalities. My difficulties involve sequencing, discrimination, and figure-ground tasks.

It was hard for me to learn the topics taught to me in my school. Although I think I was on par with my classmates as far as my reading level was concerned, it seemed as if I could not absorb the information I read.

When I was a small child, I was slow in understanding the academic curriculum. Usually, that's the first sign of a learning disability. From standard first to standard seventh, I was facing difficulties in coping mentally with the curriculum or extra-curricular activities. The other signs of learning disabilities were having a shorter attention span, shyness, and being an introvert. In the classroom, while other children seemed to effortlessly grasp concepts, I struggled to decipher simple words on the page, my mind getting tangled in a web of letters that refused to form meaning. This constant struggle left me feeling isolated, often leading to tears of frustration and a deep-seated belief that I am "not smart enough." Growing up, my parents noticed my difficulties early on, but it took time to receive a proper diagnosis of dyslexia. Even with the label, the road ahead was challenging. While my teachers tried their best, the traditional methods of learning often left me feeling overwhelmed and lagging behind. I would spend hours painstakingly completing assignments that my peers finished in a fraction of the time, my confidence slowly eroding with each failed test.

Until the age of 12, I didn't know about learning disabilities until I joined a personal class. My tutor guided me through the process of learning disabilities as she saw the difficulties I was facing in my school days.

My school's Special Education teacher made me realise that a learning disability is a commonly faced problem, and it can be fixed by giving me special attention and remedial therapy. During these sessions, I felt like the studies were simplified for me, and there were a few benefits for me that helped me not give up on my studies. Though at times I felt left out of the regular classroom, at the end of the day, those remedial sessions and my special teachers' hard work helped me fix my learning disability.

Yes, I also received unnecessary criticism in the form of jokes, like fellow students calling me LD (learning disabled) or weak, but having attended these special sessions and extra classes helped me to cope with the learning disability.

Later on, when I was promoted to the ninth grade, I had the opportunity to choose subjects of my interest.

And those subjects were as valuable in knowledge as any other subjects. My teachers and friends made an extra effort to help me cope with these vocational subjects and score good marks. Due to this learning disability, I received certain provisions at the Secondary School Certificate Board Examination. These provisions included extra time to complete my written papers, condoning spelling errors, and, of course, the choice of vocational subjects instead of studying languages like Hindi or Marathi.

With the help of these provisions, I was able to not only pass out of school but also pass out with a good percentage.

My story is a testament to the power of perseverance and the human spirit's capacity to overcome adversity. Though I faced moments of doubt, I learned to embrace my differences, finding my own unique path to success. This proves that a learning disability does not define a person's potential but rather presents an opportunity to learn and grow in different ways.

After passing my tenth, I realised that I had overcome half of my fear of learning disability. I got admission to a good college.

I can't claim to have begun my college career with the "right" attitude. My parents insisted that I attend college. I wanted to work as I needed to support my family financially, but they knew I would not be able to find a good job. During this period, studying was not my highest priority. I chose subjects that I had an interest in, made new friends, learned new subjects and the privileges of a learning disability continued in college.

Learning disability wasn't a disability for me, but it helped me to understand my capacity and pursue my goals in life.

– Daisy"

Food for Thought

Concluding Reflections for the Reader:

Dear readers,

What has it been like to look at things in the way that we have read in this book? What would it be like to reflect on these experiences? What possibilities might come from these reflections?

Would you like to share your thoughts?

Write to us at – kashmirakakalia@gmail.com

Notes

As mentioned earlier, the writing in this book is purely based on the author's experiences. This book intends to share the author's learnings from her practices, share the power of resilience, and, most importantly, spread awareness and create an inclusive environment in society.

References

Agena, J., Boecker, G., Churchill, H. (2021). The effects of stigma on students with learning disabilities and inclusive classroom practices. *The Community Psychologist, Volume 54* (3).

Corey, G. (2012). *Theory and Practice of Counselling and Psychotherapy* (9th ed.). Belmont, CA: Brooks-Cole.

Das, J. P. (1998). *Dyslexia & Reading Difficulties: An Interpretation for Teachers.* SAGE Publications.

Davis, R. D. and Eldon M. Braun, E. M. (1994). *The Gift of Dyslexia.* The Berkley Publishing Group.

Donohue. M. (2020, September 14). 10 ways to help seniors avoid social isolation. *Blue Moon Senior Counselling.*

https://bluemoonseniorcounseling.com/10-ways-to-help-seniors-avoid-social-isolation/

Kakalia, K. (2024, October 24). Decoding Dyslexia: Lyla's Story. *ImPerfect.*

https://imperfect.co.in/decoding-dyslexia/

Kakalia, K. (2024, November 8). Empowering young readers: A therapeutic approach to dyslexia. *ImPerfect.*

https://imperfect.co.in/dyslexia-therapy-young-readers/

Marshall, A. (2004). *The Everything Parent's Guide to Children with Dyslexia.* F+W Publications, Inc.

Price-Ellingstad, D., Reynolds, J., Ringer, L., Ryder, R., Sheridan, S. (2000). A Guide to the Individualized Education Program. Office of Special Education and Rehabilitative Services, U.S. Department of Education.

https://www.ed.gov/sites/ed/files/parents/needs/speced/iepguide/iepguide.pdf

Understanding the different types of intelligence: IQ, EQ, SQ and AQ https://cambrilearn.com/blog/understanding-types-intelligence-iq-eq-sq-aq

What is inclusive education? (n.d.). *Allfie.*

https://www.allfie.org.uk/definitions/what-is-inclusive-education/

White, M. (2007). *Maps of Narrative Practice.* W.W. Norton & Company, Inc.

Wooldridge, S. (2023, April 12). Writing respectfully: Person-first and identity-first language. *NIH Office of Communications and Public Liaison.*

https://www.nih.gov/about-nih/what-we-do/science-health-public-trust/perspectives/writing-respectfully-person-first-identity-first-language

Useful websites for readers:

https://divyangkalyan.maharashtra.gov.in.

https://www.education.gov.uk/iedss

https://rehabcouncil.nic.in/

About the Author

Kashmira Adil Kakalia is a mental health professional, narrative therapist, and special educator.

A versatile individual, passionate about working with people of all age groups. Her love for cooking and experimenting with food made her write a cookbook, "That's the Way to Cook," which she shared with her family and friends. She believes that sharing is caring. Inspired by technology and her nephews, who would write blogs, she had her own blog for recipes. Her daughter, who wrote haiku, also greatly influenced her. She regularly writes for community magazines and newspapers, too. Her devotion to her profession and her belief that we must share our knowledge with all led her to write this book. In this book, 'Abled Tales,' she shares the vast experiences she had with various individuals in her career of three decades.